C000181581

BNBL

Please return/renew this item by the last date shown.

To renew this item, call **0845 0020777** (automated)
or visit **www.librarieswest.org.uk**

Borrower number and PIN required.

Libraries**West**

Published by
**British Association for Adoption & Fostering
(BAAF)**
Saffron House
6–10 Kirby Street
London EC1N 8TS
www.baaf.org.uk

Charity registration 275689 (England and Wales)
and SC039337 (Scotland)

© Jeanne Kaniuk and Eileen Fursland, 2010

British Library Cataloguing in Publication Data
A catalogue record for this book is available from the British Library

ISBN 978 1 905664 34 4

Project management by Jo Francis, BAAF Publications
Designed by Helen Joubert Designs
Typeset by Fravashi Aga
Printed in Great Britain by T J International Ltd
Trade distribution by Turnaround Publisher Services, Unit 3,
Olympia Trading Estate, Coburg Road, London N22 6TZ

BAAF is the leading UK-wide membership organisation for all those
concerned with adoption, fostering and child care issues.

The paper used for the text pages of this book is FSC certified.
FSC (The Forest Stewardship Council) is an international network
to promote responsible management of the world's forests.

Printed on totally chlorine-free paper.

FSC
Mixed Sources
Product group from well-managed
forests and other controlled sources

Cert no. SGS-COC-2482
www.fsc.org
© 1996 Forest Stewardship Council

Contents

This series

Ten Top Tips for Supporting Adopters is the eighth title in BAAF's *Ten Top Tips* series. This series tackles some fundamental issues in the area of adoption and fostering with the aim of presenting them in a quick reference format. Previous titles are:

- *Ten Top Tips for Placing Children*, by Hedi Argent
- *Ten Top Tips for Managing Contact*, by Henrietta Bond
- *Ten Top Tips for Finding Families*, by Jennifer Cousins
- *Ten Top Tips for Placing Siblings*, by Hedi Argent
- *Ten Top Tips for Preparing Care Leavers*, by Henrietta Bond
- *Ten Top Tips for Making Introductions*, by Lindsey Dunbar
- *Ten Top Tips for supporting Kinship Placements*, by Hedi Argent

Details are available on www.baaf.org.uk.

Acknowledgements

My thanks to all the adopters and adopted children who have taught me so much about what it means to create family bonds through adoption – and how much courage, faith and energy are required. I am also grateful to the many social work colleagues I have worked with at Coram over the past 30 years, who have shared my journey of discovery, including Lorna Zumpe, Melanie Atkins, Norma Sargent, Jane Greenwood, Dorothy Rickard and Val Molloy.

I am grateful to Shaila Shah, Jo Francis, Elaine Dibben, Pat Beesley and others at BAAF for their professionalism and assistance at all stages of writing this book. Thanks also go to Eileen Fursland, for helping me to bring my thoughts to paper.

This book is a collaboration between Jeanne Kaniuk and Eileen Fursland, a freelance author.

Notes about the authors

Jeanne Kaniuk has been the Head of the Coram Adoption Service since 1980. During that time, the team has placed nearly a thousand children with adopters, many of whom have made use of Coram's post-adoption service. Jeanne has always had a commitment to helping those vulnerable children who are unable to live with their birth families, and who need the security of adoption. She believes passionately in the importance of providing support to adoptive families at times of need, and was involved in developing the Coram parenting skills training for adopters.

Jeanne was also responsible, along with Miriam Steele and Jill Hodges, for a research study following the development of their attachments to their adopters of 100 adopted children over the course of the first two years of their placements. This research (now following the same youngsters in mid-adolescence) has yielded important information to aid in our understanding of how children who have suffered adversity view parental figures, and how these views can be changed by living with attentive and nurturing adoptive parents.

Jeanne was awarded the OBE for services to children in 2010.

Eileen Fursland writes about social issues, particularly those affecting children, and has written a number of guides, booklets and training programmes for BAAF.
www.create-and-communicate.com

Introduction

Isobel was 48 and Hugh 56 when seven-year-old Angel came to live with them. Hugh had taken early retirement and was at home full time to care for Angel. Isobel was a primary school teacher with masses of experience of girls of Angel's age. Hugh had two adult children (a son and daughter) from an earlier marriage, and he and Isobel had fostered troubled children for the local authority for several years. They felt well prepared to care for an adopted daughter, and looked forward to putting their energies into enjoying family times with her.

Angel was petite and pretty. She had grown up in a family with a mentally ill, depressed mother and a father who was abusive towards her mother and sometimes harsh in his punishments of her as a small girl, for example, shutting her in a dark cupboard for several hours. Superficially Angel was a charming child, but deep down life had taught her not to trust the grown-up world, and she felt on one level that her birth mother had let her down badly by not protecting her from her abusive father.

Some of this was understood by the social worker who had talked to Isobel and Hugh about Angel before she was matched with them, and they had felt they understood what this would mean for them as parents. However, what they had not fully appreciated was the difference in the dynamics and expectations when a child joins the family with the hope of adoption, rather than as a foster child. As foster parents, they had sometimes felt challenged and exhausted emotionally, but they could take pleasure in their foster children's progress without the expectation of the child becoming a part of their own family. With Angel, it was different. She was pleasant to visitors and indeed charming when her social worker came to see the family. However, she had a way of belittling her adoptive mother that was very hurtful, and hard to manage over the course of time. She acquired social graces and was able to manage social situations that were less intense than family life. However, she was lonely at school where she did not have the skills to negotiate and join in with other children in a natural, playful way, and was often excluded. At home she lacked any spontaneous expression of pleasure and often seemed to deliberately spoil occasions that her new parents had planned as enjoyable outings. Life at home became increasingly stressful for them all.

The family's adoption worker understood how stressful family life was, and did her best to help Isobel and Hugh remember Angel's traumatic experience of parenting as a very small child. She helped them to think of strategies to avoid conflict, and of ways to develop Angel's self-esteem by finding little things to praise and celebrate. She also helped the parents to remember that it would take Angel a long time to trust that this family could be different, and that in order to build up a different expectation (for Angel) of being cared for, the couple would need to demonstrate that they were robust and resilient, and could accept the angry, destructive side of her as well as her pretty, charming persona.

The family were referred to a Child and Family Consultation Service where the parents had the opportunity to reflect further on Angel's needs and the impact she was having on each of them and their relationship. At the same time, some work was done with Angel on her life story.

Despite the intensive efforts of the different professionals and Hugh and Isobel's own commitment, the situation appeared to drag on without significant improvement for two years. The local authority began to worry whether this was the right placement for Angel, but everyone agreed that to move her again would be devastating, and that, despite her apparent lack of commitment to this family, she had indeed put down roots and felt that this was now her home.

The adopters felt committed to Angel, but they also began to feel trapped as they wondered how and when she would let down her defences and be able to enjoy the ordinary exchanges of affection and spontaneous expression of feelings that most of us take for granted. The pressure built up, and Isobel became increasingly depressed, and was finally signed off work by her GP, who prescribed antidepressants. The couple struggled to decide whether they could continue with Angel, and there was discussion with the local authority as to whether they would have to remove her.

The family's adoption worker provided intensive support, visiting the adopters and being available on the telephone. Finally, Hugh and Isobel decided that they really did not want to repeat Angel's previous experience of rejection and abandonment. They made a commitment to continue with their adoption plans. However, Isobel was quite unwell because of her reactive depression and needed time to recover. Fortunately, the local authority was able to find an excellent respite care foster home where Angel could be cared for for a fortnight to give her adoptive mother time to recover her strength. Hugh telephoned Angel daily, and her social worker visited her to reassure her that this was a temporary arrangement.

Although no one had ever told Angel that there was a possibility of her placement ending, it seems likely that on some level she was aware of just how much she was testing the couple's resilience and their capacity to deal with her pain and the experience of rejection, which she had so powerfully projected onto them. The fact that in the end they did not reject her, but renewed their commitment to her, seems to have finally reassured her that these new parents could be trusted after all. Once she returned from the respite care placement, there was a remarkable change in her behaviour and her ability to express emotions. She spontaneously gave her mum a hug and expressed pleasure to be home, which was in itself something of a breakthrough. This was not the end of the journey, but they had all come through a terrible trial, and felt closer to each other. Hugh and Isobel felt able to lodge their adoption application with the court a few months later, and they are all very much a family now.

This is a fairly typical story of the extraordinary commitment that many adopters demonstrate on their journey to becoming a real family for their child. This book is very much written from the stance of a practitioner who has increasingly come to recognise and respect the emotional strength and resilience of those families who put themselves forward to adopt children who have suffered a range of adversities. As professionals, our task is to try to understand the complex emotions that are engendered in these new family units, where strangers are brought together and given the opportunity to learn together how to be a family, how to be parents to a child who has endured emotional pain and rejection, and how to be a child who can trust adults to be reliable, nurturing and protective. We need an attitude of enormous respect, together with the ability to hold hope and optimism for the future, whilst not belittling or denying the real emotional struggles involved for the family. Sometimes placements do have to be brought to an end, when we have asked more of the adults – and of the child – than we realised, and more than was manageable. And if that is the case, it is important to recognise that it is generally the professionals who misjudged the situation, and made a placement that has not been able to endure, rather than blaming the adopters. A small number of adoption placements do disrupt (20 per cent was the figure named in the Prime Minister's Review of Adoption in 2000, which means that 80 per cent do not) and generally what is required of us as professionals is to have the courage to stay calm and reflective and to help the adopters to find their own way through to building a relationship with the frightened and lost child who sometimes can appear so omnipotent and self-sufficient.

This book is intended for the wide range of social workers who become involved in supporting adoptive placements, and who may have differing levels of experience of adoption. Therefore, some sections may seem self-evident to some readers. Those who may consult this book could include social workers from the local authority children's teams with statutory responsibility for the child's placement, adoption workers from placement teams, whether in local authorities or voluntary adoption agencies, post-adoption workers (based in local authorities or voluntary adoption agencies), Adoption Support Service Advisors, children's Guardians and also workers in other settings who need to understand something about the way adoption support services are delivered.

The book covers a very wide canvas and is not intended to be a comprehensive guide to supporting adopters. Rather, it attempts to describe the legal frameworks within which adoption support services are offered, and to indicate some of the underpinning principles on which a successful support service for adopters depends. These include:

- an attitude of respect for the adopters and the children, all of whom undertake extraordinary journeys with courage and hope;
- the capacity to remain positive and hold the hope which is so essential if adopters are to be enabled to stay the course when difficulties multiply and solutions are sometimes hard to find;
- the courage to face sad and distressing feelings and to be able to bear the despair and pain experienced by some children and their adopters along the way without becoming overwhelmed;
- resourcefulness and flexibility in seeking appropriate support services for adoptive families;
- steadfastness and availability – adopters need to know that they can rely on their social worker to stay the course and to be there reliably when they need support;
- awareness of the different needs and resources of different families, and an ability to work creatively with families from a range of backgrounds (cultural, ethnic, religious) and different family structures (single-parent households and couples, whether married or not, heterosexual or lesbian/gay);
- the ability to remain child-centred and to remember that the child's needs are paramount.

There are chapters on financial support for adoptive families, supporting members of the adoptive parents' wider family, including any existing children of the family, contact, managing children's difficult behaviour, and identifying resources.

The book ends with a bibliography to enable readers who want to follow up particular subjects to do so, along with a list of books which would be useful for adopters.

TIP 1

The role of the statutory framework

> *Some help was put in place without our having asked for it. We were told that because we had a child with disabilities we were "entitled" to a home help from the local authority...We'd much rather have help more directly geared to William's needs...*
>
> *(Marsden, 2008, pp 108-109)*

Adoption affects adopted children and their families at different stages throughout their lives. As children develop, issues arising from their adoption may assume a new significance, and will need to be reconsidered. For children adopted from the care system, the legacy of past adversity is likely to present them with particular challenges as they grow up. For all these reasons, the Adoption and Children Act

2002 (England and Wales, and the Adoption and Children (Scotland) Act 2007 recognised that adoptive parents and children may need support not only before and during placement but also in the years after the adoption order has been granted. Local authorities (Health and Social Care Trusts in Northern Ireland) are therefore responsible for providing a comprehensive adoption support service in their area. While new adoption legislation is under consideration for Northern Ireland, the current Adoption (Northern Ireland) Order 1987 provides the basis for post-adoption support. This, however, is not as prescriptive as legislation elsewhere in the UK.

Readers should be aware there may be differences in wording in primary legislation, regulations and guidance across the UK countries, and consequently variations in agency procedures and practice. What they have in common is a growing understanding of the value of post-adoption support and the need for a solid statutory base upon which to develop services.

Before the adoption order is made

At the matching stage, children and their prospective adopters will be assessed on their need for adoption support services (see *Adoption Support Services: an overview*, below). The subsequent support plan will be part of the placement plan (although this is not practice in Northern Ireland) and will be presented to the adoption panel considering the match of the child with the adopters.

The child's social worker should assess the child's needs and find out what support is available in the local authority where the child will be living (the receiving authority). Some of the child's needs will be met by universal services such as health visitors, play groups, nursery provision, etc. Other children might need therapy or special help in school, and finding out about the local CAMHS resources before placement is important if such a need has already been identified. Tip 8 describes ways of accessing such support.

It is important that adoptive parents understand that they will continue to be entitled to request an assessment for support at any time in the future if the situation changes or problems arise. However, the responsibility for providing and funding such help shifts from the placing local authority to the local authority where the adopters live three years after the adoption order is made (not established procedure in Northern Ireland) (except for financial support already in place and contact arrangements, which remain the responsibility of the placing local authority). If adopters feel that it is expected that they may need help at some time, they are likely to be more willing to ask for it if things do get difficult in the future. It is important to provide reassurance about this.

When children are placed with adopters through a voluntary adoption agency (VAA), they are placed with adopters in the area where the VAA operates, so a range of services will be available via the VAA, in addition to those provided by the local authority where they live. The VAA may also help to negotiate with the local authority for other services the adopters need.

Adoption support services: an overview

Under the Adoption Support Services Regulations 2005 (England and Wales) and the Adoption Support Services and Allowances (Scotland) Regulations 2009, local authorities must provide a range of adoption support services in their area to people affected by adoption, which of course includes adopted children and adoptive families, as well as other children in the adoptive family. Although Northern Ireland has the Adoption Allowance Regulations 1996, it does not have other specific adoption support regulations in place; but it is still good practice for services to be provided.

Support services are defined as:

- financial support;
- support groups for adoptive parents and others;
- assistance, including mediation services, in relation to contact between the adopted child and others, including birth parents and birth brothers and sisters;
- therapeutic services (for adopted children);
- help for adoptive parents to ensure the adoptive relationship continues, including respite care and training to meet any special needs the child has;
- help where there is the risk of an adoption arrangement disrupting

    or when it has actually disrupted;

● counselling, advice and information.

While a local authority will not necessarily provide all of these services itself – such as therapeutic services for adoptive children – it has the responsibility to access and, if necessary, fund these services.

Although adopters have the right to request an assessment of their needs for support services, there is no equivalent right to provision of support. The local authority is free to decide what support, if any, to provide to any individual, based on resources available, etc.

Support services: whose responsibility?

Many looked after children will be adopted by parents living in a different local authority. Which local authority is responsible for providing support services?

The first three years: wherever the family lives, when the child has been placed by a UK adoption agency, assessing and providing support services remains the responsibility of the placing authority for the first three years after the adoption order. (This would have to be specifically negotiated if the child is placed in Northern Ireland, as this is not yet established practice.) This includes responsibility for managing and supporting contact arrangements.

After three years: after three years from the making of the adoption order, the local authority where the family lives takes over responsibility for assessing and providing support services. However, if the placing authority provides financial support during the first three years, it continues to be responsible for this. The placing authority also remains responsible for supporting any contact arrangements.

When the child is not placed through a UK adoption agency (e.g. if the child is being adopted by a step-parent or from overseas), the local authority where the adopter lives is responsible for assessment and support throughout. If the adoptive family moves, then the responsibility passes to the new local authority.

Local authorities may also – at their discretion – provide services to people outside their area when they consider it appropriate.

Assessment

Local authorities have to assess the needs for adoption support of the adoptive child, the adoptive parent or parents and any child of the prospective adopters when they are considering placing a child. Once a child has been adopted, they also have a responsibility to make an assessment when they are asked to do so by adoptive parents and adopted children, amongst others. This usually involves interviewing them. (This would also be considered good practice by Health and Social Care Trusts in Northern Ireland.)

The assessment must consider:

- the needs of the child or person being assessed and how these might be met;
- the adoptive family's needs and how these might be met;
- the adopted child's needs, including developmental needs, and how these might be met;
- the adoptive parent's parenting capacity;
- wider family and environmental factors;
- the circumstances that led to a child being placed or matched for adoption;
- any previous assessment.

After the assessment, the local authority must tell the adopter whether or not it proposes to provide him/her with adoption support services and, if so, which services will be provided. In some cases, this may also include financial support (see Tip 9 for more information).

In preparing the plan, the local authority may have to consult the primary care trust, local health board (in Wales) or local education authority if services may be needed from these organisations.

If the assessment is being carried out at the matching stage, the plan will be part of the placement plan.

If circumstances change

There should be a review at least annually to consider whether any changes are needed in the provision of support services. Local authorities also have to review support services if there is any change in circumstances, for instance, if there is a major change in the child's behaviour. Behaviour which is manageable in a younger child may require specialist support if it has not improved as the child develops. For example, a severely disabled child who has mobility needs must have different kinds of aids as he grows in size and becomes more difficult to lift or carry. Similarly, a child who has violent tantrums might be managed in a family during the toddler years, but if such behaviour persists when he is of school age, the school and the family will need specialist support.

Where services are being provided during the placement period, this will be reviewed at the child's LAC/post-placement reviews – within one month of placement, then after a further three months and, after that, at least every six months. Support provided post-adoption should be reviewed if circumstances change.

If a local authority wants to vary or end the provision of adoption support services to someone, it must give the person the opportunity to make representations before it makes any decision.

Adoption Support Services Advisers

All local authorities in England and Wales must appoint an Adoption Support Services Adviser (ASSA) (or adoption support worker, in Scotland; in Northern Ireland a support worker may be appointed. The term ASSA will be used throughout this book). This person is the point of contact for people affected by adoption and for staff in the local authority. ASSAs consult with other local authorities, for instance, liaising between them when a family is moving to another area. They are also responsible for strategic planning and liaising with Primary Care Trusts and local education authorities regarding resources for adopted children.

In practice, the different aspects of this role are often carried out by different local authority workers. The ASSA may be the person who has most contact with service users; with someone in a senior role taking a more strategic approach in working with other organisations, although this is not always the case.

Adoptive parents can make the ASSA their first port of call for questions about adoption support services and how to access support. ASSAs should encourage adopters to access available support services, including both mainstream and specialist adoption-focused services.

Where appropriate, ASSAs should act as advocates, for example, liaising with education or health services on behalf of an adoptive family. The ASSA will generally be based in the local authority post-adoption team and that team may be the point of contact.

ASSAs also facilitate joint working across authority boundaries. The ASSA in a receiving authority will be a key contact for a local authority placing a child for adoption out of the area, although in practice, this responsibility may be delegated to the adoption support worker.

The placing authority remains responsible for assessing the child and his adoptive family's support needs for three years from the adoption order. But in some cases the receiving authority might agree to provide services and recover the cost from the placing authority.

Although it is only local authorities which are required to have an ASSA, most voluntary adoption agencies will have a person in an equivalent role, often their post-adoption worker.

Assessing adoptive families

Assessing adopters when they ask for help needs to be sensitively done.

- You or your department may already know the family well, in which case your task will be to ensure that you update information about them and their circumstances, and concentrate on getting a full picture of the current difficulties that have caused them to approach the department. It is also important to find out what form of support they think would be most effective. In some cases, the family may be very clear about this, for example, one adoptive mother had a stroke and became wheelchair-bound. Her husband had to continue caring for her and their adopted children as well as working. They needed help with child care. Obviously, for an adopted child, any such family crisis is likely to reawaken deep-seated insecurities, so the kind of arrangements that might suit another family were not suitable for this family, who needed help in the home after school to care for children till the adoptive father returned. In other situations, it will require more exploration to assess how to support a family where, for example, the adopted child is showing behavioural difficulties at school. This might require not only a meeting with the parents, but also with the class teacher and possibly the SENCO to discuss the difficulties, and to help the school understand those issues that are adoption-related. The solution might involve negotiating with the school for additional classroom support, or might require close home–school liaison, or might result in referral for further assessments.

- If your department does not already know the family, the assessment will need to be more extensive, as you will have to obtain the child's history as well as to get to know the family and their strengths. *Practice Guidance on Assessing the Support Needs of Adoptive Families* (DfES, 2005b) gives guidance on using an adapted version of the *Framework for Assessment* for use with adoptive families, although you should be selective about which aspects you need to focus on. It is important for adopters to feel that you understand the urgency of their situation, and that you spend time understanding the current situation and also the context of the child's early life. You will also want to understand what strengths the adopters bring to the situation, and what supports there are (both professional and also via family and friends) in their wider network.

Local authorities do have some discretion in how they allocate their funds and the support they give in individual cases. The fact that adopters have the right to request an assessment of their need for support services but no right to actual support sometimes leads, not surprisingly, to a certain amount of dissatisfaction. However, once the local authority has agreed to carry out an assessment of support needs, reasons must be given in writing for deciding not to provide support. These situations often call for persistence in making the case, networking with other professionals in the child's school, the child's GP and so on. If expensive resources are needed, there may be a case for joint assessment and funding, including education and health services.

After the adoption order

When a child is placed and settled with an adoptive family and any adoption support has been agreed, it is not the end of the story. At different times in the child's development, issues can arise which mean that the child and family need more support, which might lead them to contact the local authority. There are also a number of adoption support organisations throughout the UK which adopters can contact for advice and information.

Some families join support groups for adopters in the area where they live, even though they are still in touch with the placing authority for support for the first three years. It is a good idea to encourage this, as it means they are likely to get to know people in their local adoption support service and become absorbed into the local network. This could make it easier for them to access appropriate help if their child develops problems in future. Some local authorities run support groups for adopters, as does Adoption UK (see Tip 10, Useful Resources), which runs them in many areas throughout the UK. Adoption UK's website also includes a message board and a buddying system which can provide support. There are also a number of adoption support organisations throughout the UK which adopters can contact for advice and information.

Life moves on and social workers leave, so...

- Make sure you give adopters a copy of important documents and reports. They are entitled to the information pack at placement, including: a full copy of the Child's Permanence Report (in England), Child's Adoption Assessment Report (in Wales) or Form E (Scotland and Northern Ireland), which includes all names and addresses of the child's birth family members; the Adoption Placement Report (including the adoption support plan and arrangements for contact); and the Adoption Placement Plan. This is not practice in Northern Ireland, where they receive an agency summary including the child's personal and health history, and a record of the agencies involved. They should also have received the child's life story book.

- Before the adoption order is made, it is also important that the adopters receive a "later life letter". This is written by the child's social worker to the child, to be read when he is a young adult, to give him a fuller picture of his background and the reasons for his adoption. If the letter is written by the social worker who knew his parents, it is important to give a brief description of them. This letter will build on the simple version provided in the life story book, and answer more of the young person's questions. It is important to be truthful and to give a clear picture of why his birth parents could not care for him, but also to give these difficult events some context which helps to explain his parents' difficulties. It is helpful to end on a positive note, and recall the time when the young person's adoptive parents first met him, and how delighted they were – giving confirmation of the young person's place as a member of his adoptive family. (The agency summary in Northern Ireland generally encompasses all these details.) This is an important document, and the ASSA should be able to give advice about composing it.

- Encourage adoptive parents to feel they have a relationship not just with their social worker but with the agency as a whole.
- Provide easy ways for adopters to stay "in the loop". Support services such as study days, support groups and newsletters provide a continued link to the agency. Adopters who have kept in touch are more likely to ask for help when they need it.
- Keep full records so that adopters or adopted children who may contact the agency years later can be given the information they require.

After three years

Approaching the right person

Make sure parents know that, if they ever need help from their local authority, they should approach its Adoption Support Services Adviser (ASSA) or adoption support worker. If they need to be referred to the children's team, it would be helpful for the post-adoption worker to be involved in this. Many workers who work with children in need will lack experience of adoption. Social work teams dealing with "children in need" often operate different thresholds for intervention, and may not necessarily appreciate the circumstances of the adoption, or just how desperate adoptive parents can feel or what they may have endured before asking for help. An adoption support worker, on the other hand, will understand that adoptive relationships can be quite fragile. They will know that if adopters are asking for help, they should take it seriously.

Adopters' sense of entitlement to support is often quite weak – because they have been assessed and approved to be adopters, they may feel they ought to be able to manage. They can suffer from an acute sense of failure and guilt which makes it hard to ask for help – so by the time they do so, they are often very stressed. Adopters often feel blamed by professionals, so try to make it clear that you understand they are bearing the brunt of the impact of the child's early experiences. Build alliances and try to develop a network of supportive professionals and agencies which can help the family.

The teenage years

Everyone recognises that adolescence can be a difficult time, even for teenagers who have grown up in a happy and supportive birth family. Many teenagers who were adopted as children are faced with, firstly, the emotional legacy of their troubled early life and of having two very different strands to their identity, often powerfully played out in challenging behaviour towards their adoptive parents. Secondly, all of this, of course, is overlaid with the anger and rebellion that typify the teenage years. Many adopted teenagers go through a difficult period as they try to work out who they are, sometimes rejecting their family's and society's values and testing parents and teachers to the limit.

During adolescence, a small but significant number of children develop severe behaviour problems. In particular, those who experienced early rejection, neglect or abuse and who were adopted as older children may be emotionally and behaviourally disturbed, angry and hostile towards their adoptive parents. Sometimes they reject their adopters and over-identify with their birth family. Children who experienced domestic violence and who were the victims of sexual abuse or who had inappropriate sexual experiences before coming into care may retain confused ideas about their sexuality. In adolescence, some of these young people may act out sexually in ways which put them at risk and cause enormous concern to their adopters.

Troubled teenagers are easy prey to harmful influences. They may, for example, truant or be excluded from school, get involved with gangs, crime and violence, turn to self-harm or substance misuse or develop eating disorders. Not surprisingly, it can be hard for even the most committed adoptive parents to hold the situation together.

Adopters need specialised support

Social workers who are not experienced with adoption may misunderstand the dynamics of the situation, which are influenced by the young person's earlier abusive or neglectful experiences in their birth family. Other social work teams may have very different expectations of the families they work with, or different thresholds for intervention. If they are lacking in experience of adoption, it can be easy to underestimate the gravity of the situation for the adopters, or to misunderstand the messages they and the child are trying to convey.

Adoption or adoption support teams, on the other hand, can understand what lies behind the child's "acting out" behaviour. It is important to recognise how stressed adopters can feel – even if they are resourceful and resilient – after many years of caring for an emotionally demanding child. Conveying that you understand and respect what they have managed is enormously important in establishing a working relationship.

Approaching an experienced adoption support worker will ensure that families are likely to feel understood. Families having serious problems need to be able to access advice and support that takes into account the psychology of adoption.

Taking the long-term view

We know from studies of late placement adoptions…that problems in children do not hold to a constant pattern, but may abate and then re-emerge afresh or in a different guise at a later developmental stage. This poses a problem for services characterised by the need to open and then close cases, or geared to brief, time-limited interventions. Continuity of service over many years is hard to deliver given inevitable changes of staff and of service organisation and perhaps varying resource levels. From the service providers' point of view, it is difficult to balance carrying responsibility for a continuing group of problematic placements as well as the ongoing business of recruitment, assessment and preparation

> *of potential adopters. But without such continuity, adopters can find it frustrating to have to undertake fresh negotiations each time problems become too pressing to manage. Services need to be available to respond to crises as they arise and when family patterns are not so entrenched that...the placement is heading for disruption.*
>
> (Rushton, 2009)

The challenge facing adoption support workers is to provide the services that will help adoptive families to "hang on in there" through tough and troubled times whenever they occur. **In this stressful job, it is also vital that support is also available to workers, from their colleagues, their managers, and their agencies as a whole.**

Key points

- Ensure that you know the law and what adoptive parents are entitled to – they will need your advice and advocacy skills.
- The support given to adopters should be reviewed regularly, to ensure that adopters' and children's needs are still being met. This is especially the case if there are any changes in circumstances.
- To understand what support this family needs, you have to know the adopters, the child and their circumstances.
- Encourage adopters to seek support in their area – local adopter support groups can be invaluable.
- Bear in mind that adopters may need to contact your agency after you have left your position. Ensure that records on file are full and up to date. Ensure they have full information, and a larger relationship with the agency, instead of just with you as their social worker.
- Other social work teams with less experience of adoption may misunderstand the needs of adoptive families, and the gravity of the situation when adopters are asking for support. Be available to help adopters to convey their needs.

TIP 2

Recognise that adoption radically changes adopters' lives

It's stating the obvious, but it's a fact: adoption changes your life! You can't just absorb a child into your family without changing your lifestyle. You have to give up certain things, you have to make financial adjustments, you have to cope with emotional pressures and deal with changing relationships. I think we grossly underestimated the impact adoption would have on our lives.

(Marsden, 2008, p 98)

When a child is placed with adoptive parents, to the social workers involved it may feel like the successful end of a long process – but to the adoptive parents, of course, it is the first day of the rest of their lives. And adopters often face practical and emotional challenges that other new parents don't.

Taking on someone else's child is very different from having your own. Adopters have to parent a child whose early life involved experiences that will have affected her in ways they may never fully understand. Learning to live with an adopted child, particularly if that child has difficulties, involves a huge adjustment. And learning to love someone else's child does not always come easily.

Adopters have come through the long and gruelling process of assessment and preparation. They may feel that they have been well prepared and know what to expect – but of course the reality of having a child in your life and your home, 24 hours a day, seven days a week, can come as a shock.

Particularly for those who have been childless up to this point, the full-on experience of looking after a child or children means that every aspect of their life changes overnight. They may feel they have no time or space to manage their own lives and priorities or to do the things they used to enjoy. They may feel ragged and exhausted through having many broken nights and expending so much energy – both emotional and physical – on looking after the child. Indeed, adopters often became ill at an early stage in the placement.

The child may also trigger strong emotions in the adopters – intense sadness at their difficult early years, anger and frustration at their behaviour, guilt at their own reactions – which may take them by surprise. In some cases, adopters may find that their own memories of difficult episodes in their childhood are brought back to their minds by their child's experiences. They may need reassurance that these feelings and reactions are normal, and can be managed.

Adopters often feel they should be grateful – that they have been granted the child they longed for, so they have no right to say that it's hard. If you are supporting an adopter or adoptive couple, you need to help them understand that it's OK to find it difficult. Make it clear that you will not judge them if they need to let off steam, complain or cry once in a while when it all gets too much.

If adopters feel they are not coping well, it may help if you reassure them that it is not unusual to feel the way they do. Without trivialising what they are going through, you can tell them: 'Other families have told me that they have found it a really hard time and it takes longer than you expect to adjust.' Reassure them that everyone makes mistakes and that they will learn as they go along. Encourage them to be kind to themselves.

> *Laquayah, who is black like myself, came to me as a very disturbed child who sought a lot of attention. She'd been in foster care all her life, and I think attention seeking was her survival technique. She took over my life. Fortunately I was divorced and my two adult birth children had left home, so I could give her the attention she craved.*
>
> (Carol, quoted in Sturge-Moore (ed), 2005, p 107)

Often adopters don't receive the same level of support that other parents do when they have a new baby. Other parents may not fully empathise with what adopters are going through because they haven't experienced it themselves. (See Tip 6 for more on involving family and friends in the adoption process and in providing support.)

If the adopters are a couple and one of them has gone back to work, the one who is left at home to care for the child may become overwhelmed and lonely without adult company. This is of course also true for single adopters. Whereas mothers with a new baby might have met other new mothers at NCT or other post-natal classes or at the clinic, new adoptive mothers often lack these networks. They can feel left out when other mothers discuss what their labour was like or some incident from their child's baby years and they can't easily join in. Encourage adoptive parents to think about where support might come from – do they have friends who don't go to work, or a local toddler group which they could attend, for example, to get to know some other parents? There may be a local support group for adoptive parents that they could join.

Encourage all adopters – especially single people and those parents who are at home full-time – to build some "me-time" into their week for relaxation, exercise or to pursue interests or activities they enjoy on their own or with friends.

Some adopters are known to suffer the equivalent of post-natal depression. You should be aware of this possibility; if adopters seem to be having these problems, simply accepting the reality of the feelings may be sufficient to allay them. If such difficulties persist, you should advise the adopters to seek advice from their GP.

'Will we ever learn to love him?'

We were deemed good enough to adopt. Twenty months later we were introduced to a four-and-a-half-year-old boy. He was gorgeous, funny and bright. We took him home. Within a month we realised that we were totally unprepared for any child, let alone one with behavioural problems... Two years on we reached breaking point. We were being terrorised by a six-year-old.

(Hirst, 2005, p 16)

Sometimes adopters don't immediately take to the child. They might have been anticipating feeling a rush of love when a child was finally placed with them – and feel alarmed and disappointed when this doesn't happen, especially since the adoption is such a huge commitment. It is not unusual or unnatural for adoptive parents not to feel love for their child at first. It can take a long time to develop a real emotional connection, and professionals need to be reassuring and give the adopters space to find their feet, rather than pressurising them into moving towards the adoption order before they are ready.

It sometimes helps if you reassure them that in many cases the connection grows through the everyday practical routines involved in looking after the child. Often parents have to carry on with the day-to-day caring while they wait for their feelings to "catch up". However, if the doubts persist, it is important to give the adopters space to express their concerns and to consider whether some additional support is needed (see Tip 5). Ultimately, if such feelings do not lessen, there may need to be a decision about whether this placement is really right for the child.

Couple relationships

For a couple, becoming a family of three or even four overnight can unbalance even the strongest of relationships. Even in birth families, the arrival of a new baby puts a great strain on the parents' relationship and requires couples to re-negotiate their roles.

Quite often an adopted child will build an attachment with one parent first, ignoring the other parent. One parent may feel swamped by the child's demands, while the other parent may feel useless or rejected. It is natural for a child to build an attachment with one parent at a time and both parents will need help to manage their feelings. Help the "left-out" parent not to take this personally and to find ways to support his or her partner.

Often it is the adoptive mother who senses rejection from the child, possibly because of children's feelings of confusion and anger towards their birth mother, which get projected onto their adoptive mother. Whatever the reason, for adoptive mothers who have waited so long to form a bond and love the child – and be loved by her – it can be hard to bear.

Another common scenario occurs when one parent is at home, perhaps having been battling for much of the day to get the child to co-operate. When the other parent arrives home from work in the evening, the child suddenly becomes happy, delightful and eager to please. The favoured parent may assume that he (or she) has a better knack of managing the child, which can be extremely galling for the parent at home, who is feeling bruised after a hard day. In adoptive families, this situation is often compounded by the child working out negative feelings with one parent and being more ready and able to enjoy the company of the other.

Couples need to find time and make the effort to communicate and share their feelings about these tensions, so that they can support each other rather than feel divided. Helpful strategies might include suggesting that the parent who is at home all week has some time off from childcare at the weekend, allowing the other parent to take on the childcare role by themselves, at least for part of the time. This takes some pressure off the home-based parent, giving him or her time to relax. The parent who works may develop more insight into how hard it is to look after a child at home all day, as well as the opportunity to build a relationship with the child through shared experiences.

The reality is that the new parents will have to prioritise the new child and to organise their lives around her needs for some time. This requires the parent/s to have time to be at home and the ability to empathise with how confusing the move must be for the child.

Brothers and sisters

If there are already children in the adoptive family, they will have been waiting for their new brother or sister with excitement and probably some trepidation. Relationships between adoptive parents can often be unbalanced when they adopt a child. But where there are existing children in the family – whether birth children or other adopted children – family relationships are also likely to be strongly affected. Children already in the family will find their parent/s preoccupied with the newcomer and may feel jealous and pushed out. Even teenage or adult children can feel excluded or jealous, although this may be an unexpected reaction for their parents and even for themselves. It is important that the children already in the family also have some quality time with their parents during these early days. (See Tip 6 for more on supporting brothers and sisters and involving the wider family.)

Key points

- Adoption is a huge adjustment for all concerned. The difficulties of this adjustment can be overlooked by social workers, who are coming to the end of a long process. Be aware that the adopters may be finding the transition to parenthood more problematic than they expected.

- Difficult emotions can be triggered by the child's arrival – reassure adopters that this is common, and support them to manage these emotions.
- Love often grows gradually between adopters and child, rather than happening overnight. Support adopters through this process.
- Be aware, and ensure adopters are aware, of the need to pay attention to changed family dynamics – both between the partners (if the adopters are a couple), and with other children in the family, if applicable.

TIP 3

Create a supportive relationship with adopters

> *We felt very comfortable with our social worker. She was very friendly and supportive and...was not under the illusion that anyone can be the perfect parent.*
>
> (Sarah and Georgina, quoted in Hill, 2009, pp 197–198)

Avoid implying criticism or blame

As a social worker, you need to create a relationship in which adopters feel they can be honest and discuss their concerns without you judging or blaming them. Help them to realise that you won't blame them if they are struggling. Because adopters have to go through so much in order to be approved, they will be very sensitive to anything that feels like criticism. They may already be feeling like failures if they are struggling to cope – and any implied criticism is likely to be counter-productive, and to make them defensive. Adopters may be allocated a new social worker when their child is placed, which can make matters even more difficult for them – in the stressful early days of a placement, a new social worker may not be seeing adopters at their best. It is important that you do all you can to ensure that your relationship with the adopters is built on trust, openness and honesty.

However well prepared adopters are before a child is placed, preparation can never be the same as the reality of coping with a child who is upset or angry. Part of your role as a social worker is to empathise with adopters and to acknowledge that they have taken on a hugely difficult task. Emphasise that the child arrived with his own particular needs and difficulties, and that it can be hard to stay positive when you feel ground down and dispirited – this will make for a more open and helpful discussion. If you can assure the adopters that their worries and struggles have been heard, they are likely to be more open to seeing some positives in the situation as well.

Take concerns seriously

Social workers sometimes try to reassure adopters who are concerned about tantrums, rejecting behaviour or wakeful nights and so on by saying that it's a normal part of a child's development. This can feel quite belittling to adopters who are struggling to understand and respond to children who have had lives that are anything but normal.

Comments like this may leave adopters feeling that nobody understands them or takes them seriously. It can deter them from asking for help, or in the future they may escalate their descriptions to try to convince the worker that there is a real problem. You need to do two things: convey your concern about the adopters' experience; and try to understand what the child's behaviour is communicating so that together you can consider how best to respond to the child.

If an adopter tells you that their child's behaviour is worrying or upsetting them, this is significant information – even if, on the face of it, you don't think the behaviour sounds particularly extreme. It may be that the adopter's limited experience with children means that they are unsure what behaviour is to be expected at different developmental stages, or that they are worried about whether their child is meeting developmental milestones – in these cases, they will need more advice and information from you about child development and how this relates to their adopted child. On the other hand, it could be that it is not just the child's behaviour but his powerful underlying feelings that the adopters sense and find so disturbing – if this is the case, they may need advice from you about the importance of conveying that they know the child sometimes feels angry, confused or sad, rather than reacting to the child in a negative way.

A seven-year-old girl, Jill, would be charming and co-operative when the social worker visited. However, when at home with her adoptive mother, she was rejecting and dismissive, for example, she would ask for a particular dessert then refuse to eat it, saying that her previous foster carer knew how she liked it prepared. Over the course of time, this made her mother feel worthless and depressed. She found it helpful when the social worker pointed out that Jill had been treated as worthless all her life, and she had found a way to let her new mother know just how bad she felt inside.

For adopters, the issue of seeking help can be complex. In a 2007 survey (Sturgess and Selwyn, 2007) of 54 families who had adopted children, although a third of adopters were happy to receive support services, others were reluctant to seek help for fear of seeming to have failed, or not wanting to feel blamed, or because they preferred to struggle alone.

Maintain professional boundaries

Social workers are generally aware of the importance of maintaining a professional role and boundaries. However, this may feel more difficult to maintain, and even unnecessary, when working with adoptive families. Whereas many other families that social workers encounter may have very great difficulties in managing their lives, adopters are generally capable people. It may seem natural to treat the adopters as friends and share some of the worker's experiences as either a parent or even as a fellow adopter.

However, doing this is not likely to be helpful to the adopters. Your role is not to be a "buddy", and it can be demoralising for an adopter to hear that you have succeeded (or even failed) when they are struggling. They want you to attend to *their* situation.

If you want to draw on your own experience, it is better to say, for instance: 'I know an adopter whose child used to hate sleeping in his own room at night, so the whole family had sleepless nights. The adoptive mother didn't want to let him sleep in her bed, as she thought that would start a pattern that would be hard to break. In the end she solved the problem by putting a mattress in her room for him to use if he couldn't get to sleep.' That is much more helpful than saying 'When my son wouldn't sleep in his own room, I used to...'

It's also not helpful to chat about your own family and family life when the adopter is struggling with a child who has not yet learned to sit still in the classroom.

Taking on the role of a "friend" could make it difficult if, at some time in the future, you have to say something uncomfortable. This doesn't mean being *unfriendly* in attitude, of course – it simply means understanding your role and demonstrating your support by your interest in this family's experience.

Make it clear who the parents are

Many children who have been looked after are very quick to come up to strangers, wanting to play, show their toys and make friends. They have been looked after by so many different adults that they don't expect to have a particular attachment to their mother or father. Indeed, being able to relate to many adults is often a survival skill for these children. The social worker must take care not to get drawn in by the child's approaches in a way that undermines the child's developing attachment to the new parents. Both the child and their adoptive parents need you to reinforce the idea that *they* are the parents. (For more about this, see Tip 6.) Of course, there will be times when the child's social worker will need to spend time with the child to discuss how she feels about her new family.

Empower the parents

As a social worker, your role is to help the parents to reflect on how things are going and to support them in coming up with strategies to use with their child. They will need to have their confidence built up, so it is important to offer praise for any small achievement, such as establishing a routine for meals, kicking a ball in the garden before tea or spending time playing with the child at bath-time. Although you may at times find that an adopter is struggling when you visit, it is important to avoid stepping in and taking over any aspect of the parenting role. Instead, concentrate on helping the parents to reflect on what they have achieved and how they can manage current problems.

Build trust

> *My social worker is lovely. I feel at ease when I'm talking with her. She takes me the way I am.*
>
> *(Caroline, quoted in Sturge-Moore (ed), 2005, p 47)*

You will hope that the adopters feel able to let you know about any difficulties so that you can support them. But some adopters are afraid that, if they admit to problems, you may think them incompetent. You will therefore have to be explicit about reassuring them that it is usual for adopters to experience problems from time to time, and you will not see it as a failure if they confide in you.

Invite adopters to agency events

Inviting adopters to events such as study days, support groups and social events which are open to all adopters approved by the agency/local authority keeps the lines of communication open and provides adopters with a way to keep in touch. It also gives them a low-key way to raise concerns if and when they need this – they may find it easier to approach a worker in this way rather than by phoning up to say: 'There's a problem.'

Key points

- Avoid implying criticism or blame – adopters are in a difficult situation and will be doing their best. Reassure them that you support them in this and help them find strategies to manage the difficulties.
- Take adopters' concerns about the child's behaviour seriously and try to understand what the adopter is experiencing – such concerns could point to a need for further assessment of the child's difficulties.
- Retain professional boundaries in your work with adopters – this makes it easier to advise them without seeming to judge their actions.
- Empower adoptive parents by helping them reflect on what they have achieved with the child, as well as on how they can solve current problems.

TIP 4

Encourage adopters to be optimistic but realistic

I think it is vital to look at why you are adopting, what your own vulnerabilities are, and what you are really wanting from the relationship. The social worker was very good at helping me to discover some of these things and she made a brilliant match.

(Lorraine, quoted in Hill, 2009, p 173)

'Will he ever learn to love us?'

No one would take on a child without the hope of developing a close relationship with her, even if they understand that it will take time.

The long-term impact of childhood abuse and neglect can be hard to predict, but we know that it can make it difficult for children to trust adults and develop secure attachments. All adopters will have learned about the likelihood of attachment difficulties, but it is natural for them to hope that their love, care and nurturing will put things right for their child.

Social workers would not place a child without sharing that hope at some level – at the same time as recognising that difficulties often persist for many years. But, of course, it is never possible to know how an adoption will turn out or how long the journey may be.

Children with attachment difficulties may function well in their foster homes. Foster carers offer a "safe haven" without necessarily making many emotional demands on the child, and may not see it as a problem if the child does not bond with them or vice versa, since they do not relate to the child as a permanent family member. Therefore, the child's difficulties in forming an attachment may not have been identified prior to the adoption placement.

But in adoptive families, parents want to develop a close, warm, spontaneous relationship with their child. Not surprisingly, many adoptive children do not understand about loving and secure relationships, and do not expect adults to be consistent or nurturing. It can take them a very long time to make attachments, which can be hard for parents to bear. Adoptive parents hold so much hope for the future, but they have to live with uncertainty. It is important for the child that their parents are able to maintain a steady and supportive relationship despite the difficulties. They also need to hold on to the belief that their care is providing the child with the foundations for a different future. Offering false reassurance to the parents is not helpful, but giving them the opportunity of talking to adopters who have survived similar experiences is one way of providing realistic support. (Adoption UK runs support groups in many parts of the country and also has a web-based message board where adopters can seek support from other adopters about particular problems.) Talking to adopters about research into long-term outcomes can also be helpful – see the information on David Howe's research later in this chapter.

If the adopters become disappointed or disillusioned, they may need help to keep going. They are on a journey of discovery about their child. Some helpful messages would be that, although no one may ever know exactly what all the child's earlier experiences were, she may be "acting out" these experiences in her relationship with the adopters: they will be the ones who will know her best. She needs adults who won't give up on her – because that's what has happened to her before. The child needs to know that the adopters will "stay the course". Until children have experienced stability in their lives over a long period, it will be hard for them to learn to trust adults – and some children test out adults very thoroughly.

Reassure the parents that if they can offer routine and consistency along with warmth and opportunities for play and fun, they are giving their child the best possible chance at recovery. Experience and research show that children do benefit from the security of adoptive family life, and over time the quality of their relationships will improve. (See Tip 5 for more information about attachment issues and promoting attachment.)

The long-term view may be rosier

Relationships can and do change. A study by David Howe of the University of East Anglia (1996b) shows that many adoptive parents eventually enjoy a more intense, caring and reciprocal relationship with their adopted child than they would ever have thought possible during her difficult and demanding teenage years.

Researchers asked adopters about their current relationships with their grown-up adopted children and also about their relationships with them during adolescence. The study covered 100 children who were at least 23 years old at the time of the study.

Howe categorised the children into three groups, according to the type of care they had experienced before their placement.

- Those who were adopted as babies (six months or younger) and had experienced little, if any, adversity in the quality of their pre-placement care apart from being transferred to the adoptive family. Howe classed these as "baby adoptions".
- Those who were placed at older ages, usually with a history of neglect, abuse or rejection from an early age. Most had experienced several changes of caregiver and several years of social

work involvement. Howe called these "poor start/late adoptions".

- The third group comprised adopted children whose life and care began reasonably well for the first few years and it was not until later on that their care deteriorated and they experienced adversity. They often experienced one or more episodes of foster care before finally being placed for adoption. Howe called these "good start/late adoptions".

Howe asked parents what their children had been like as teenagers. There were highly significant differences in the scores for ten measures of adolescent problem behaviour (self-mutilation, eating disorder, lying, truancy, exclusion from school, running away from home, substance misuse, theft from home, offences outside the home and violence against a family member) between the three groups. Most of the children adopted as babies experienced no major problem behaviours, according to their parents. In contrast, children in the poor start/late adoption group exhibited an average of 2.62 problem behaviours.

However, at the time of the study, by which time the children were all young adults, 93 per cent of parents viewed the adoption positively and said their relationship with their child was good.

The biggest improvement was found in the group of children who had had adverse experiences in early life and were adopted relatively late, i.e. after babyhood. Although some of these children had problem behaviours throughout their childhood, adolescence was a time when their angry and challenging behaviour tried their parents to the limit. In this group, only 38 per cent of parents felt that their relationship with their child had been positive in adolescence; but 67 per cent reported that their current relationship was positive.

Those who did manage to "ride the storm" (which could last several years) often found that their very insecure, hostile and angry children slowly began to develop an increased sense of security and self-confidence. They stopped fighting with their parents and during their 20s, seemingly for the first time, were able to accept their love without feeling confused, angry and anxious.

In a few cases, relationships did not recover and parents and children had lost contact or conflict continued (although the longer-term outcome could still improve for this group as well – the research only followed them up to a certain point in time).

The message from those parents who finally achieved more relaxed relationships with their grown-up children is "stick with it" and "stay in there".

But many also felt the need to make one final point. To help manage the times of great stress, parents said that what is needed is support and advice from people who not only are experts in children's development but also have a sophisticated and skilled understanding of the psychology of adoption.

'Will she ever catch up with other children?'

The social worker tells you about the possible horrors that could lie ahead, such as attachment problems, behavioural difficulties, uncertain prognoses and so on. You take it all in, but you harbour an assumption that you will be different from everyone else who has struggled with these things; you will buck the trend.

(Marsden, 2008, p 98)

Adoptive parents often have high hopes that they can help their child reach her full potential and that she will achieve the same as any other child. They are often extremely focused on how they can help her catch up with other children of the same age and make up for any developmental delay she may have suffered as a result of her early experiences.

However, it is counterproductive to try to "hothouse" the child. All children need to be allowed to be children – and this is absolutely vital for a child who has been neglected or abused and has never had "ordinary" opportunities to experience reliable, consistent care.

You may need to explain to parents that it's better for children to have opportunities to play than to be struggling with extra homework. It may help to remind them that in some countries children don't even start school until the age of six; and that if children are emotionally settled, they will have the mental energy they need to concentrate and do their best at school. Play is the way children learn about the world they live in; whether messy play, painting, pretend play, or playing alongside other children, all these are activities that help a child's development. Children who have had little opportunity to play may be rather limited in how they can entertain themselves, and sometimes it is better to start them with toys that seem young for their age to let them catch up on missed opportunities. Learning to play co-operatively with other children is a big step, and many older adopted children will need an adult present to ensure that their child manages to share and co-operate, as you would expect to do for a toddler.

Whatever the parents' aspirations for their child – and helping children to achieve their potential is a good thing – it is unproductive to put pressure on a child to achieve academically or in other ways if she is still struggling to cope with the effects of early adversity.

You may need to encourage the parents to have appropriate expectations – for some children, it is an achievement if they manage to sit on the carpet at story time at school. This would be a good opportunity to praise the child for her efforts. Adopters need to be on the lookout for things to praise to build their child's self-esteem. It is no good waiting for big steps – every little achievement needs to be welcomed. They should celebrate every small thing their child learns to do, whether this is sitting at the table for meals or learning to do up her shoes, even if it happens much later than for most other children.

Many adopted children are hampered by poor self-esteem. Praise and encouragement are great motivators and finding things children can enjoy and do well is vital.

'Will she ever behave like other children?'

Most babies have the experience of being the centre of attention in their family. Everyone delights in them and their parents constantly try to anticipate their needs and keep them safe and happy. They learn that they are special. But so many children who have been looked after have never been special, have never been anyone's priority, have always been left out or ignored, or worse.

For example, adoptive parents playing a board game with their adopted child may well be disappointed when the child kicks the table over because some other child has won the game. They say: 'She needs to learn how to lose.' What you need to help adopters understand is that these children need to learn how to win! They need to experience succeeding and enjoying positive attention before they will truly be able to play co-operatively. Similarly, it is not helpful to expect a child to be good at sharing – whether it's toys, sweets, food or adult attention – when she has never had enough attention for herself. The idea of helping a child to practise doing things she finds difficult could be extended to social skills such as "practising sharing".

Some children who have been neglected or abused may find it difficult to "own up" and be truthful about their actions, and this can be worrying for the parents. It is important to help them understand this behaviour in the context of their child's earlier experiences. Reassure them that it does not mean their child is "bad", but that she has learned a strategy to cope with a frightening and unpredictable early environment. Encourage them to be tolerant and patient, rather than punitive, as they help their child practise telling the truth.

Children need to learn the difference between right and wrong, but adopted children also need to learn that they won't be harshly punished or rejected if they admit to doing something wrong. The child may fear that an angry adult will do something terrible, or will stop loving them. Children who have always been loved and cherished never believe their parents will stop loving them, so admitting to misdemeanours is less threatening for them. It is important to remember that this is not the case for children adopted from the care system, who may live with an unexpressed fear of being rejected yet again and having to move to a new placement.

Support can sometimes mean persuading the family they have something to give...Undefined "support" for adoptive parents can mean an amorphous and largely passive response hardly likely to help in managing severe behavioural problems. On the other hand, we know that adopters can have their confidence dented by a hard-to-manage child and say that simple recognition of their struggles, reminders of small positive changes, and a strong dose of approval when they are full of self-doubt can be very restorative. Genuineness is what matters. False reassurance and empty optimism will be quickly detected and ignored...Support can sometimes be a matter of giving hope and persuading the family that they have something to give to the unrewarding child even though they may be feeling defeated.

(Rushton, 2008, p 267)

Key points

- Provide adopters with information about the outcomes for other adopted children – through adopter support groups, publications or research. This can help them to be realistic but optimistic about their child's future.
- Help adopters to see the long-term view – it may take time before their child can love them.
- Helping children to achieve their full potential and to "catch up" with their peers is important for adopted children, but so is giving them the time to be children. Adopted children may need to act younger than their age for a while to allow them to feel secure in their new family.
- Help parents to understand their child's behaviour in light of their early experiences, and to understand that this behaviour can be changed. The idea of "practising" new social skills can be helpful to adopters as well as children.

TIP 5

Managing a child's challenging behaviour

> *[The teachers] gave us the impression that sufficient TLC would put everything right for him. I was embarrassed when I tried to talk about attachment difficulties to anyone. It felt like an admission of the most fundamental failure.*
>
> (Royce and Royce, 2008, p 34)

How early trauma affects children's development

Babies who have experienced good enough care in their early months and years are likely to have secure attachments to their primary carer(s). Alongside that, as they develop, they will develop the capacity for self-regulation of their emotions, managing ordinary levels of stress and frustration without becoming overwhelmed, for example, being able to settle down with a cuddle and a story and go to sleep at bedtime. However, for many adopted children, the abusive early care or extreme neglect they may have suffered in their first year of life will have affected their neurological development and the level of cortisol, the stress hormone, in their system. They are likely to have insecure or disorganised attachments, and will not have the expectation that adults will be reliable or will take care of them.

By the time these children are placed with adopters they are often unable to relax and are hypervigilant – subconsciously on the lookout for danger all the time, even when they are in a safe environment, and unable to unwind and go to sleep at bedtime. They will often react to changes in routine or to minor stress, such as an unexpected visitor, by becoming overwhelmed. Tantrums are common and can be both fierce and prolonged.

Some children develop different strategies for dealing with stress. They may appear to be unresponsive and unaware of what is happening around them, which may seem as though they are not interested. However, this is more likely to indicate that they have learned to cope with overwhelming stress by "dissociating" or cutting themselves off from what is going on. These children can be quite out of touch with ordinary interactions with people for much of the time. Alternatively, other children will be easily upset, clinging and irritable.

All these reactions may have been the best solution a vulnerable baby could find in a dangerous situation. But once the child has been placed with a family which is trying to nurture him and help him experience being safe and cared for, these reactions are counter-productive and have the effect of keeping the new parents at bay. This can feel extremely rejecting to the adopters, who will need a great deal of support while they get to know and understand their child.

Children who are rejecting towards their new parents may appear rather different to social workers and others who see them for a limited period. This is because the child may have learned to cope with adults on a superficial basis, whereas adopters are seeking to build an intimate relationship, which feels much more threatening to the child.

It is important not to undermine the adopters by appearing to suggest that they have got it wrong and that their child's reactions are normal, which may seem to be the case if the child is friendly to the social worker. One of the most important sources of information about the child's capacity to build a new relationship is the way he responds to his new parents and how he makes them feel. What they describe about their feelings is therefore highly significant.

Making the child feel safe

Adopters need to establish a predictable environment with routines that will gradually help the child to feel safe. They will also need strategies to help them reach out to the child who appears self-contained and independent. What children who have been let down by adults desperately need is the experience of being cared for – of being able to depend on an adult to look after them. However, if their previous lives have taught them that adults are unreliable, neglectful or abusive, they may be frightened by their new parents' attempts to be close to them. Adopters need to be encouraged to reach out to their child (without being intrusive or overwhelming), to offer care in small ways, for example, a drink at bedtime, or ruffling the child's hair if a hug feels unsafe to him.

It is important that adopters who have a child who seems unusually independent don't assume that this child is fine, and that they do not need to pay him much attention. Rather, the message should be that this child is at risk. He has learned to act as if he can manage on his own, but inside there is a frightened little boy who really needs a parent to care for him.

For example, 18-month-old Danny was good at feeding himself and playing on his own. His adoptive mother's friends said, 'Aren't you lucky! He is such an independent chap. He will be ready for nursery soon!' Fortunately, his social worker could see that Danny was really not ready to begin separating from his mother. She encouraged her to continue with her adoption leave (as had been planned before placement) and to take every opportunity to do things with or for Danny. As Danny began to trust that his adoptive mother would be there for him, he became quite clingy for a while and had several very disturbed nights. His social worker realised that this was an important part of his bonding with his adoptive mother. She pointed out that by waking at night, Danny was seeking reassurance that his mother would be there for him when he felt frightened. His adoptive mother was then able to experience her new little boy's dependency as a special and precious stage in their new relationship, rather than as a problem.

Talking about feelings

Adopters also need reminding that adopted children may often have had scant experience of talking about feelings, and may have little emotional vocabulary. It is very helpful to children if the adults can name feelings and talk about the ordinary events of the day, as a way of building up a scaffolding of communication. For example, if a ringing doorbell causes the child to cringe or hide under the table, you could suggest that the adopter says: 'That was only the doorbell, but it gave you a fright when it rang. You are safe here, it is my job to look after you. Let's go and see who is at the door.'

Remind adopters about attachment difficulties

Emma was allocated as our new support worker...She was less well informed than Rose and Joy but was making it her business to understand attachment.

(Royce and Royce, 2008, p 48)

In their preparation courses, adopters will have learned about the range of difficult behaviours that adopted children can show and the reasons why so many of them have problems with forming relationships and behaving appropriately. Nevertheless, until they experience the reality of living with a child who has such difficulties, it is hard to really understand the impact this can have. It can be reassuring to remind adopters that what they are coping with is not uncommon for adoptive families, and perhaps to remind them about their preparation course.

Adjusting expectations

All adopters will have hopes and expectations about their child and also about how they will manage as parents. It is often a shock to any new parent when their life is taken over by the demands of a child who still feels like a stranger, and adopters will struggle with feelings of exhaustion and confusion as they try to establish new routines, get to know their child, and learn what he enjoys or finds difficult. It often takes a while to unpick the triggers that upset a child or result in tantrums. It is important to spend time talking over difficult situations with the adopters, so that together you can discuss strategies for managing the behaviour.

REGULATING FEELINGS OR HELPING A CHILD TO CALM DOWN

Anja had adopted a seven-year-old boy who became overwhelmed if his routines were altered. Finding a supply teacher at school, for example, could result in tempers and tears all day.

After school on one such occasion, Anja said to him: 'I can see that you feel upset and that makes you feel very cross. I think it will help you to calm down if you sit at the kitchen table with me, and colour this whole piece of paper in green.' By doing this she avoided sending him to his room, which might have felt like a rejection. She gave him a simple, repetitive task to concentrate on, which was well within his capabilities, whilst also acknowledging his feelings and that he needed help to calm down rather than a punitive reaction. In this situation, she could be near him, doing something in the kitchen, available but not in any way crowding him – and indeed, he did calm down so they could then do some cooking together.

Adopters also have complicated feelings!

Adopters often expect that they will quickly fall in love with their child after all the waiting and the time and energy they have expended on becoming parents. It can be a shocking experience if they don't have feelings of love, and even more so if they find themselves resenting the child's impact on their lives. These guilty feelings can be hard for adopters to admit even to themselves. On the other hand, they may worry that if they keep the child in their family without feelings of love, that they will be "shortchanging" them in the longer term. The reality is that for quite a substantial number of adopters, feelings of love are long and slow in coming.

A child who has been placed beyond babyhood will have a formed personality and will already have had experiences which make him more difficult to care for. It is important to accept that the adopters may have negative feelings and to normalise this by saying that this happens to many adopters, who sometimes find a side of themselves they had not met before, and which they don't like.

Often the way forward is for the adopters to continue looking after the child, while waiting for their feelings to "catch up", without the adopters being hard on themselves and feeling like a failure. It is helpful to build in positive experiences with the child, and for the adopters to ensure that they are looking after themselves and having a break from childcare – perhaps the other parent can take over (if they are a couple), or maybe another family member can babysit for a few hours.

When things are going wrong

Adoptive families should be trusted and treated as responsible parents unless there are concerns about safeguarding the children. Above all else, when

> *adoptive families are in a state of crisis, they must be taken seriously. Their views need to be heard, their perceptions have to be taken into account and their pain has to be acknowledged.*
>
> *(Carr, 2007, p 131)*

For some adopters, particularly those who have adopted a child with serious emotional and behavioural problems, life can seem to turn into a series of crises. Adoption may have left them feeling inadequate, and wondering whether they will ever be able to establish a harmonious family life. They are likely to experience deep feelings of stress, frustration, unhappiness and anxiety. It is important to remember that children who are difficult to live with may not present the same problems for those outside the family. You should avoid minimising the child's problems when talking to the adopters – people experiencing such levels of distress need to feel supported, not criticised. Some of the foundations for helping families at such a time are listed below.

- **An open and supportive relationship** in which adoptive parents can talk to you about their worries and feelings is essential. Having a social worker who is reliable and visits regularly can in itself give the adopters the sense of being supported. Tip 3 gives some tips on building this kind of relationship.
- **Listening skills** are essential. It is important that the adopters feel you are giving them your full attention, and that you understand what they are saying. Adopters often struggle to articulate exactly what it is about their child that is so problematic, and it is important to understand the impact of the child's behaviour on them.
- **Understanding attachment difficulties:** having an understanding of why the child's behaviour is so difficult is important as it helps the adopters to feel more in control, to be able to empathise with their child and rationalise some of their own hurt feelings when he rejects them. Tip 4 discusses this further.
- **Learning to break the negative cycle**: unfortunately, when

children are repeatedly angry and rejecting, it is easy to be drawn into responding angrily and starting a negative cycle. From the child's point of view, anger may seem more familiar than positive attention, and more under their control. Adopters need help to avoid getting trapped in negative reactions. One excellent strategy for building a positive interaction with their child is the technique of non-directive play, described later in this chapter.

'Why weren't we told?'

Sometimes adopters who are having a tough time claim that social workers didn't tell them the whole truth about their child. They may feel deceived; that the full extent of the child's problems was kept from them in order to ensure his adoption. It is important to listen to what they have to say without becoming defensive and to acknowledge how desperate they feel. Once you have established that you are taking what they say seriously, you could suggest that it is hard for anyone to know exactly what a particular child will be like in an adoptive family, for a number of reasons:

- When he was assessed in his foster home, the child may have seemed very different. Many foster carers are managing several difficult children and may not offer much individual attention, so a child who is distrustful of adults can "blend in" without too many emotional demands being made of him. This may result in the child's real difficulties remaining hidden until he meets people who really do want to establish a close relationship, i.e. when he is placed for adoption.
- Adoptive parents are likely to have very different hopes of the child's relationship with them than the child's foster carers did. Although the increased one-to-one time and nurture may be what the child needs on one level, on another level it can feel intrusive and threatening. He may react badly to this and try to keep the adopters at a distance.
- Each time a child moves from one placement to the next, it is likely to affect him in some way. Moving into an adoptive family represents another disruption on top of all those he has experienced before. In this situation, the child may feel very vulnerable and defend himself by acting as if he doesn't care.

- Sometimes it may be helpful to look back at the child's file and connected paperwork. Information may be recorded which has not made its way into later reports.
- If a child is adopted after his earliest months, there will always be many unknowns about his past life. It is impossible to discover all the aspects of a child's experience in his birth family or with other carers which may affect him later in life, so there will always be some gaps in the information recorded.

SPRING TIME AND MEMORIES

Karen, aged eight years when placed, always seemed to have crises in the spring. She would become unpredictable, having terrific tempers and trashing her bedroom in reaction to what seemed very minor upsets. One day, after she had been in her adoptive family for two years, she said to her adoptive mother: 'Mum, you know, I've been thinking, it's the spring time now, and all the daffodils are flowering. I remember that when I was first taken into care, the daffodils were flowering. Now when I see daffodils it makes me feel sick and miserable. But it is something I've only just remembered now'.

The adults could not have guessed that the sight of the daffodils upset this little girl so much, and she herself did not make the conscious connection until she had been in her adoptive family for two years. That she was now able to explain this was a real tribute to how much she had grown in her ability to make sense of her feelings, to recall the past and to trust in her adoptive parents.

Social work support for children

If you are the child's social worker, you will be visiting up until an adoption order is made, and it is important to listen to what the child is saying and also to act as a channel of communication between the child and the adopters.

If, for example, the child has talked about some difficulty at school or about being worried about his birth mother, you should explain to the child that it is really important for his adoptive mother to also know how sad he has been feeling. You should then go with the child to talk to their adoptive parents about what you have discussed.

Sometimes the only thing you will be able to do with some of the sad feelings is to acknowledge them. For example, if a child wants contact with someone who is likely to be very destructive, it is important to acknowledge their feelings of loss, but to add something like: 'The wise judge said that it was important that you had time to enjoy being a child and to learn how to be a family with your new mum and dad. I know you worry about your birth mother (or whichever term the child and adopter use), and she has her own social worker who visits her to see that she is all right. Your mum will write to her every year to let her know how you are. When you are older – maybe when you are 18 years old – your mum will help you find your birth mother, if that's what you want.'

Problem-solving with adopters

If the adopters are upset and worried, your role as a social worker is to create a calm environment where they can bring their own understanding and insight to the surface and arrive at their own conclusions and decisions. In this context, you may be able to feed in some thoughts and ideas, as long as you give them plenty of space to voice their ideas first.

It is important to convey the sense that change is possible. A reflective discussion where you both acknowledge the problems and try to tackle whatever the difficulty is – perhaps by breaking it down into separate, more manageable sections – can encourage a positive approach. You should be prepared to listen and ask questions with a view to understanding and empathising with the adopters' views rather than in order to solve the problem or give unequivocal advice. It is important not to generalise by saying 'All children go through phases like that' or 'My own daughter was just like that when she was a similar age'. This may give the impression that you haven't understood how hard it feels to care for a child who has difficulty in trusting adults and who makes you feel like a failure.

Adopters can also find it irritating when they are trying to explain how desperate they feel if their social worker keeps trying to explain why their child behaves like that. There is a time for explanations, but not when the adopter needs to offload their frustrations, because this may give the message that their feelings don't count.

There are several suggestions in this chapter for strategies that adopters might try in order to shift the relationship with their child in a more positive direction. Discuss with the adopters what they would like to try doing differently to manage their child's behaviour, and agree a plan.

You should reassure the adopters that you will be there to support them as they take the next step. You should always set a date to meet again and discuss how the plan is working out, and to think together about what else needs to happen to ensure that the child continues to settle and that the adopters build confidence as parents.

Parenting courses for adopters: strategies for positive behaviour management

If adopters are struggling with their child's behaviour, it might be helpful for them to attend a parenting skills course. Such courses aim to help parents feel more confident, increase their understanding of their child and to augment their "toolkit" of positive strategies to use with him or her.

- There may be parenting courses available locally, run by the local authority, schools or voluntary organisations. Sharing experiences with other parents is a valuable part of the learning. Some parenting courses are designed specifically for adoptive parents.
- A programme called *The Incredible Years*, by Caroline Webster-Stratton, has been adapted for adoptive parents by Coram and the Anna Freud Centre. Based on attachment theory, it seeks to develop positive interactions as a step towards building secure attachments. The course runs over 12 weekly sessions, and is available through several adoption agencies and some CAMHS. It emphasises helping adopters with ideas about play and praise, behaviour management, and building positive interactions. The book of the same name which accompanies the programme

(2006) is packed with good ideas, and would be worth providing for adopters. (See Tip 10 for more information.)

- The course *A Piece of Cake* is run by Adoption UK (a self-help organisation for adopters). The course consists of five whole days, and focuses on teaching adopters about attachment theory as a way of understanding their children's behaviour, as well as giving strategies for behaviour management.

The two courses above have the advantage of being specifically designed for adopters so that participants benefit from sharing their experiences with other parents who can identify with the complexities of adoption.

- A course called *Fostering Changes,* by Pallett and colleagues, was developed at the Maudsley Hospital, London, in 1999 to provide practical advice and skills-based training for foster carers looking after children with difficult and challenging behaviour. These skills are also useful for adoptive parents. *Managing Difficult Behaviour* (Pallett *et al*, 2008) is a handbook of tips and techniques from the programme for parents or carers to use at home.

Some of the approaches used by these programmes include the following:

- **Building positive interaction through play:** parents should be encouraged to put time aside on a regular basis – even as little as 10 minutes a day – for special time with their child. If this is given over to **non-directive play** (see below), the child can have the parent's attention for that time, and the experience of being able to make choices and be in charge of how that time is used.
- **Giving rewards and incentives:** adopters can target and encourage particular behaviour by giving social rewards, such as praise, encouragement and positive attention. Adopters can also reward the child in a systematic way using star charts and small tangible rewards. It is important that rewards and stars are given readily for small achievements, rather than used as a way of trying to ensure several days of good behaviour. If the child does not feel he can achieve a star, he may try to sabotage the system.
- **Reinforcing good behaviour:** an emphasis on avoiding giving negative attention where possible, by concentrating on the positives and praising even tiny things.

- **Avoiding rewarding inappropriate behaviour:** attention is a powerful motivator for a child and some children would rather have a telling-off than no attention at all. So ignoring bad behaviour – adopters withdrawing their attention from the child briefly – is sometimes a better idea than telling him off.
- **Improving communication** by making requests and give instructions positively rather than shouting and getting cross.
- **Setting limits and boundaries and using sanctions:** it is particularly helpful if in a calm moment the adopter can discuss with the child what the rules are, and what the consequences will be of misbehaviour. The adopter needs to put the discussion in the context of wanting to help his or her child to manage his behaviour more successfully, not of wanting to punish him.

Adopters shouldn't be asked to implement all these ideas at once, but you could discuss what might be a helpful place to start, and then agree that the adopters will try one or two strategies on a regular basis. This needs to be for a limited period – one or two weeks – followed by a debrief with you, as the social worker, and then making a new plan with new goals. Goals should be small, specific and achievable, for example, sitting at the table at teatime, rather than a more general "being good".

Non-directive play: a powerful technique to help children

When adults play with children, they very often try to direct the way in which the child plays, making suggestions or trying to teach the child new things. Because adopters are aware of all the experiences their children have missed, they can be particularly keen to teach and guide in this way. However, this approach does not allow the child's creativity to develop, nor for them to experience being in control in a safe way. In contrast to this, non-directive play is child-centred. The parent tells the child they will have a special 10 minutes play time each day when the child can choose what to do. The parent's task is to give his or her attention to the child and to allow him to take the lead, gently commenting on what he is doing (descriptive commentary) but not asking questions or making suggestions.

An example of descriptive commentary

Imagine an adult is with a child who is playing with a farm set. Here are two possible ways in which the adult might comment on what the child is doing.

1. 'I see you are playing with the pigs. You've put all the pigs together. Now you're putting the big pig in the barn with the cows and the dinosaur. Now you're bringing the farmer along in his tractor. He's coming into the field... You're making the farmer pick up one of the cows...' and so on.
   In this example, the child can experience having the full attention of his parent, which builds attachment between them.
2. 'Let's put the pig in the field. What colour are pigs? Do you know what noise a pig makes? You should give him another pig to be friends with. No, let's not have that dinosaur on the farm – you wouldn't find a dinosaur on a farm, would you? Why wouldn't you? Now put the farmer in his tractor.'
   In this example, the child's feelings of incompetence are reinforced by his parent's controlling behaviour.

This technique provides the child with positive attention at a time when they are behaving appropriately, and the "reward" of this attention reinforces their good behaviour, whilst also giving the child the experience of being their parent's priority for that time. Many adopted children have missed out on being special to anyone for most of their lives, and it is particularly helpful for them to have this experience. Adopters have commented on what a powerful tool this is and how much it can improve their relationship with their child.

When things go badly: voicing the doubts

Despite everyone's efforts, major problems sometimes persist and adopters may become very discouraged and negative about the child. In these cases, it is important to have a frank discussion and to allow the adopters to express their feelings and to discuss what the possible outcomes may be.

Sometimes it is a relief to adopters if the social worker makes a comment about adoptions occasionally not working out. In difficult situations, adopters are likely to have very mixed feelings and whilst one part of them will want to keep going, another part may feel defeated. If the social worker raises the possibility of ending the placement (not as a threat, nor as a definite plan, but as something that can be thought about and discussed), the outcome is often that the adopters end up feeling more committed to the adoption. This can lead to a decision to try a different approach and some new strategies with the child. Once adopters have voiced these kind of feelings, it is important to reassure them that you will keep in touch to discuss how things are going and review how they are feeling at an agreed time, possibly after a month.

This might also be the time to refer the family to CAMHS for assessment and consultation, perhaps with negotiation with the CAMHS team for an early appointment. It would also be important to ensure that the CAMHS referral includes information about the child's early history and why he has such emotional problems, so that the clinic understands that the adopters are struggling to help a child who came to them with severe difficulties. If this is not made clear, adopters have sometimes felt as though they were being blamed for causing the child's problems.

However, once the social worker raises the possibility of ending the placement, sometimes the adopters may acknowledge that they really don't feel they can continue. If this is the case, it may be that the placement is not sustainable. However, there should still be a period of reflection before a decision is made. Holding a professionals' meeting, which includes the adopters and all the professionals involved in the child's life, can be a useful way to review the placement, looking at the progress made by the child since joining the family as well as the difficulties, and offering some further supportive measures. Whilst these discussions are ongoing, it is important to avoid blaming the adopters and to keep the lines of communication open.

RESPITE CARE WAS A TURNING POINT

Steven, aged seven, was neglected by his mother until he came into care at the age of four. He was underweight, had delayed speech and development, and no experience of regular meals or bedtimes. He was placed with an experienced foster carer who had several other children, and responded well to positive attention. However, he remained a voracious eater, not aware of when he was full. He became attached to his foster carer and told his social worker that 'She cooks, cooks, cooks, and I eat, eat, eat,' which indicated how anxious about being fed he had been.

When he joined his new family (Maggie, 48 years and an accountant, and Albert, 52 and a civil servant) as the only child, he missed the other foster children, and it became clear how he had depended on them to keep himself occupied – he had almost no capacity to entertain himself. He couldn't watch the television unless Maggie or Albert sat with him, and couldn't engage in imaginative play. The couple arranged for friends to visit so that he could play with other children, but he lacked the skills to play co-operatively. At school he was upset by any change in routine, and had several tantrums where he kicked other children or teachers.

Steven was clearly emotionally still a toddler, needing the one-to-one attention of a familiar adult to supervise his play and peer interactions. The school provided him with a teaching assistant for 15 hours a week, to give support at key times, and he joined a small group for twice-weekly reading sessions; this helped him to cope better with school. At home, progress was very slow, as he still needed constant attention and followed his new parents around, which they found frustrating.

After six months, Maggie's mother became ill and was admitted to a hospital three hours drive away. Albert took time off work to meet Steven from school when Maggie was visiting her mother, but Steven reacted badly, having several severe tantrums and trashing his room. When Maggie returned, he would not acknowledge her. He also began to have more tantrums at school. Maggie found it particularly hard that Steven had no empathy for her feelings about her mother.

When the social worker visited, they explained that life

with Steven had become an unremitting battle. The social worker acknowledged their difficulties, and that Maggie's mother's illness had been an additional blow which was seriously depleting Maggie's already-stretched reserves. She added that sometimes adopters realised that they had taken on too much, and if that was the case it was important to discuss it. However, she also explained that to Steven, Maggie's current preoccupation with her mother would resonate with his early experience of a mother who ignored him, and make him anxious about being rejected again. She said that if they did want to continue she would help them to find support, but that it was important to understand how they felt and what they wanted to do.

The couple were very honest in saying that caring for Steven currently felt like a job in which they were trapped. However, they also acknowledged that they had made a commitment to him, and they felt it was their responsibility to find a way forward. They felt encouraged by their worker's acceptance of their feelings, and also by the possibility of support.

Their social worker suggested finding someone reliable to meet Steven from school, making this part of his routine and so providing support for them as well. She also suggested a referral to the local CAMHS so that Steven's underlying feelings could be understood. When a carer was found, the social worker helped the adopters to explain to Steven that although Maggie had to visit her sick mother, that did not mean that she was not still his mum. To make sure he would be looked after, they had found a kind lady, Isabel, who would meet him from school three days each week, and look after him till his parents got home. This reassured Steven about his place in the family, and his tantrums lessened. The adopters found the CAMHS therapist very helpful in thinking about why Steven reacted as he did. Over time, Maggie and Albert developed their confidence, which made Steven feel safer. He began to enjoy doing some things on his own without adult supervision, such as watching children's television after tea.

The adopters had felt supported by their social worker's acknowledgement of their feelings and by her giving them permission to think about the placement ending if they could not continue. At the same time, she offered them an insight into Steven's past experience and the impact of Maggie's absences on him. Alongside this, she offered practical support in the form of an after-school carer (part-funded by the local authority). She also realised that this couple needed the additional support of the local CAMHS clinic, which they found helpful.

When a placement disrupts

> *If social services had supported us, and respected our concerns... who knows, there might not have been an unhappy ending after all.*
>
> (Carr, 2007, p 120)

Adoption is a remarkably positive intervention, and statistically only about 20 per cent of adoption placements break down (Performance and Innovation Unit, 2000). That means that 80 per cent do not break down, which is an excellent outcome compared to other forms of care. However, a breakdown of any adoption placement is always extremely painful, and the adults need to focus on supporting the child through this time.

Once a child has been placed for adoption, everyone involved in supporting the placement should make every attempt to ensure that the adopters get the support they need to ensure that the child settles and makes a good attachment. However, sadly we do not have a crystal ball, and building close relationships is not based on science. Despite our best efforts, some placements are not successful, and the adopters feel that they are really not able to live together with the child as a family.

If, despite everyone's best efforts, it really feels as though this child cannot be accepted or cared for in a way which feels warm and appropriate, it may be necessary to move him. Sometimes this happens when adopters ask for a child to be removed. At other times the adopters may want to keep trying to build their relationship with the child, but the local authority may feel that the situation has become damaging, and that the best decision will be to move the child. This decision should never be reached without a great deal of soul-searching, as every move will create another separation and disruption in a child's life.

In most cases, the child's social worker should talk to the child with the adopters to explain that he will have to move. This is because it is terribly painful to talk about such a situation, and the social worker can ensure that careful thought is given to the explanation the child is given for the decision to move him, and that the message is consistent. The explanation needs to be truthful, and should not leave the child feeling responsible. Sometimes it can be best to say something like: 'Everyone has worked really hard to become a family together, but we are all very sad that it has not worked. It seems Mum and Dad were not ready to be parents and they are really sorry. It is not your fault.'

When you talk to the child, it is essential that you can tell him where he will be moving and that a timescale has been agreed with the adopters. Giving the child some information about where he will be going is important. You should also speak to the school and explain what is happening. Some teachers arrange for the class to give the child a good luck card, or to write and send good wishes after the move.

Generally speaking, once the child knows that he has to move, everyone in the adoptive family will feel very raw and upset, and the child needs to move within two to three days. If possible, the child should visit the new placement before moving. If this is really not possible, the child should be given a photograph of the new carers and some information about them. It is best if there can be a couple of days for him to say some goodbyes. The child should be moved by someone he knows, and to have the reassurance of seeing a familiar adult (preferably his social worker) regularly once he has moved to his new placement.

After the child has moved, the adopters should be asked to write a letter for the child to say goodbye, and to make some positive comments about the things that were good, or the things they liked about him, and to wish him well for the future so that he has something to hold onto and read at a later date. The child also needs photos of who was in the family and of any special events he attended. He may not want to look at these straight away, but in future years it might help him to fill in some gaps. It is important for you to keep a spare copy of this information, in case it is lost or destroyed. It is important that the adults take responsibility for the decision to end the placement and that the child is not blamed.

As well as caring for the child, it is important that the social worker conveys to the adopters that their feelings are also important. No one comes into adoption expecting to let a child down, and it is extremely painful for adopters to feel that they have in some way added to the distress experienced by the child they hoped to adopt.

It is vital that, as the social worker, you have support yourself during such a painful time, and one of the things that needs discussion are your own feelings of having let the child down. Everyone is likely to feel partly responsible, but it is unhelpful to blame anyone. No one wanted this outcome, and although it will be important to learn any lessons from the experience, that is not the same as apportioning blame.

Within about two months, a disruption meeting should be held, where the history of the placement can be discussed in the context of revisiting the child's earlier life experiences. The adopters should be invited to attend the meeting together with the professionals involved and an independent chairperson, who has not shared any responsibility for the placement. This discussion often sheds more light on the nature of the child's difficulties and helps to inform plans for his future care. It should also provide an opportunity to draw any more general lessons so that future practice is improved.

Adopters who have experienced a disruption will feel extremely upset, both about the child whom they have lost and also about their own life plans to build a family by adoption. Indeed, it is like a bereavement in many ways. Although another adoption is not automatically ruled out, most adopters would feel very worried about repeating such an experience. It might be difficult for them to accept counselling or support from their adoption agency, but they should be offered support either by the agency or via some independent counselling.

Key points

- Ensure adopters are aware of the ways in which a child's early experiences can impact on his behaviour, and discuss with them how to manage this.
- Despite what they may have learned on their preparation course about attachment difficulties, these can still be a shock for adopters when they encounter them in their adopted child. Reassure them, and discuss problems and solutions with them.
- Reassure the adopters that it is OK for them to have mixed feelings towards their child in the early months.
- Ensure they are looking after themselves and having breaks from child care if possible.
- Having an open and honest relationship with the adopters can help them to feel supported and to take in your advice about managing the child's behaviour.
- Simply being there for and empathising with the adopters can be supportive. Sometimes they may need explanations or suggestions about their child's behaviour, but at other times they may just need someone to listen to their problems.
- A number of parenting courses are available. If the adopters are having serious problems, think creatively about what could best help them, and if a local course is not available, provide use of the books recommended and discuss specific strategies with the adopters.

TIP 6

Support other family members

> *I told them from the start that my sister would look after him from school till I come home...it's worked out all right and Jake's got two new families for the price of one.*
>
> *(Single parent adopter, quoted in Argent, 2004, p 14)*

When a new baby is born, friends and relatives often rally round with congratulations, offers of support and sympathy for the broken nights. There are cards, flowers and presents. Many people will have been through it themselves, so they understand what it is like.

But how many new adopters receive cards? Adoption is a much less familiar situation and people are often unsure what to do and how to react.

Adopters have often waited a long time for their child and they don't want to seem to be complaining, but they can feel just as ragged as any other new parent. Meeting the intense demands of incorporating a child into the family is just as hard work and sometimes even more exhausting than looking after a newborn baby. They also face uncertainty about how long it will take for their child to settle and adjust and for them all to feel comfortable together as a family. This is especially true with older children who have never learned to trust adults and who often test out their new parents before they can begin to feel safe.

So adoptive parents do need support and understanding and practical help, just like any other new parent. But they also need space to establish a relationship with the child themselves before she is drawn into lots of other new relationships with extended family and friends. Family members and friends may be excited themselves, and very ready to welcome the new child. However, they need to take their lead from the adopters about how best to support the new family.

Helping the child learn who is mum or dad

Adopted children often haven't learned to form close relationships. Their lives in care may have taught them that relationships don't last and that it is important to take what attention or affection you can from any available adult. They can therefore be quite indiscriminate with their affections and may be just as happy relating to an aunt or the next-door neighbour as to their adoptive mother or father. They will need to learn over time to make a special attachment with their new parents, and to understand the appropriate ways to relate to close family members and friends as opposed to strangers.

Adoptive parents may need to be supported by you in explaining to their own parents that their new grandchildren first of all need to learn to trust their mum or dad. In the early stages, it should be the parents, not the grandparents, who the child is encouraged to go to when she is upset or wants something. The same will be true with other family members.

Difficult behaviour

> *When my brother and his wife adopted Cindy,*
> *they were over the moon. Then she started all this*
> *business with screaming if she didn't get her own*
> *way. She clings to my sister-in-law, won't leave her*
> *alone for a minute...It's embarrassing because she*
> *behaves like a baby though she's a big girl.*
>
> *(Uncle of adopted girl of nine, in Argent, 2004, p 49)*

Older adopted children are often harder to love and respond to than a new baby. They can be hard to integrate into a family – they can lack social skills and may not be used to playing with other children or sharing. Because of their early life experiences, there are many skills that they will need help to develop. It can be hard for people outside the immediate family to know how to relate to them, particularly if they are very demanding or are competitive and antagonistic with other children.

Adoptive parents may find that their children are more difficult and have more tantrums than their friends' children. This can put a strain on friendships when families get together, and adopters can be disappointed when they sense that their friends are avoiding inviting their children over to play with their own children.

There are many ways in which you can help the adopters to gain the support and understanding of other family members.

- Some adoption agencies run a preparation day for family and friends of adopters, which can be a very positive way to help these important members of the network to understand some of the pressures faced by adopters and how to support them.
- Suggest the use of books targeted at family and friends, for example, *Related by Adoption: A handbook for grandparents and other relatives*, by Hedi Argent, or *Welcoming Children into your Neighbourhood*, by Jane Espley (both published by BAAF).
- Another possibility is to give the adoptive parents a letter which

talks about adoption in straightforward language for them to show to people who are important to them. Below is an example that is provided by Coram Adoption Service in London.

TO FAMILY MEMBERS AND FRIENDS OF NEW ADOPTIVE PARENTS

This is a letter to try to explain how you might best be able to support your friends and family who are in the process of adopting children.

From years of working with children who are placed for adoption and from research, we know that children often suffer a severe emotional reaction to having to move from the foster carers and the home that is familiar to them, to their adoptive homes. Most children who are adopted in this country nowadays are not tiny babies, but are older children. They may have had unhappy experiences with their birth families and they will have spent time in a foster home, where they may have become attached to their foster carers. Then they have to move again to adoptive parents who have made a commitment to bringing the child up as their own child.

Adoption offers children a new chance to have the love and security of a family, which for a variety of reasons they have missed in their birth families. However, it often takes children a long time to settle into their new families and really believe they are there to stay. These children may have lost trust in adults. Some children react by being much more grown up than their age. They want to pretend they do not need parents to look after them and comfort them when they are upset. Some children are much too friendly with strangers and reject their new parents. They can be frightened of getting too close and losing someone all over again. Some children go back to being very babyish and refuse to do things their new parents know they were able to do before. As you can imagine, looking after children at this time is very hard work for adoptive parents and their children's behaviour can be very distressing for their parents at times, which needs to be acknowledged. All of us need to support parents in the complex task of building a family through adoption so that their children can have a safe and loving family life.

Adopted children who show difficult behaviour are not being purposefully naughty – they are very distressed. They have to learn all over again the real meaning of belonging to a family. Ordinary things that you can take for granted and your children understand, adopted children will not understand without it being explained, often many times.

It would be very helpful to adopters if, when you are in their company, you take any opportunity to help their children understand that their mummy and daddy are in charge of what happens to them. For instance, if a child should ask you for a drink or a biscuit, it is important to say to the child, 'We'll just ask your mummy/daddy if it's OK for you to have this now'. If the child comes to stand or sit beside you, it is helpful if you say, 'We had better let your mummy/daddy know you are here'. It would be good if you encouraged them to sit beside their mummy or daddy, so that they know where they belong. It is important that you do not pick children up or sit them on your knee without checking that their parents feel OK with this. Many children living in adoptive homes do not understand that their mummy or daddy will always have their child in mind because that has not been their past experience and they will need time to learn how to trust their new mummy and daddy. It is very important for children to build solid relationships with their adoptive parents before they begin to make relationships with the wider family and friends.

Thank you for taking the time to read this.

Yours sincerely

- Either before or early on in the placement, you could offer to meet with grandparents, other family members and friends to explain how they can best support the new parents. This is an opportunity to explain something about the experiences an adopted child may have had (without sharing the child's private information) and the impact on the way the child behaves. This can lead to a discussion about how to support the adopters.

Here are a few practical suggestions.

1. Providing practical help like cooking extra meals that can be kept in the freezer, helping with the ironing, etc, will make life easier for the new parents and free them up to spend more time getting to know their child or giving their birth children some individual attention.

2. The new mother or father may not be completely confident about their role, so tread carefully. Don't take over tasks or react as if you know better than they do – instead, encourage them to develop confidence.

3. It's important to confirm to the child that Mum and Dad are the important people: they are the ones who will comfort her when she's upset, decide whether she can have a biscuit and take her up to bed at bedtime.

4. Respect the adopted child's right to privacy. Adopted children are sometimes treated as if they are "public property" and people may ask very direct questions about why they have been adopted. Obviously, the child's story is personal information which is private, and the adopters need to consider what they will tell others, and how to help their child deal with other people's curiosity by saying something like 'I don't want to talk about it', 'That's private', 'My mum says I don't need to tell people if I don't want to' or 'My other mum couldn't look after me, so I came here to be adopted'. If family members know that the child has been told how to deal with unwelcome questions, they can support the child if this happens when they are around.

If problems arise later in a placement, you could offer to facilitate a similar meeting for the family and close relatives and friends. This is an opportunity for people to explore their feelings and for you to explain possible reasons behind the child's difficult behaviour.

Relationships between children in a family

Children generally experience sibling rivalry and jealousy when a new baby brother or sister is born – and just like a baby, an adopted brother or sister will need a lot of attention and care.

Having to accept a new brother or sister – someone who, in many cases, has considerable "emotional baggage" and may not be particularly easy to get on with – can demand a lot from other children in the family. Consequently, the problems of sibling rivalry are often more acute in adoptive families.

The children already in the family – whether by birth or adopted or fostered – still need to feel special and have times when they receive individual attention from their parents. It is important that adopters plan to make time for this and that they talk to their children about their feelings about having a new brother or sister. If their existing children can have a role in helping the new child, this can assist in building a relationship between them. However, the new child might be extremely clingy with older children or might be quick to fight with other children, so the adopters need to be prepared for this and ensure that all the children in the family have space and are protected if necessary.

When an older child is adopted, children already in the family might perceive the child as breaking the rules and getting away with things that are not normally allowed in the family. This may be because the parents have decided to turn a blind eye to some behaviours while they focus on the really important issues for the child. Children, even teenagers, can feel outraged at the perceived "double standards" and complain vociferously that it's not fair. Children may also be distressed if an adopted child is verbally or physically aggressive towards them or their parents.

Encourage parents to sympathise with and acknowledge their children's feelings that things can sometimes seem very unfair or difficult, rather than being dismissive about this. They also need to explain that 'Annie needs to practise being part of our family and it will take time'.

It would be helpful for you to prepare the parents for this kind of thing. They need to think about how to help their children understand why the expectations won't be the same for the new child, while she is learning so much about becoming a part of this new family. Also, remind the parents that it is important to acknowledge to their children how hard it feels at times.

There may be other adopted children already in the family. If the children have very different contact arrangements, it can be painful for the one who doesn't have contact. For this reason, social workers often avoid placing a child into a family where she would have very different contact requirements from other children. However, this is not always the main consideration, and even if arrangements are expected to be similar, things can change. For example, if a sibling is traced by the local authority at a later stage, a child who had no contact may suddenly be offered sibling contact. This could create a disparity between the children, and adopters sometimes find they need to manage such unforeseen situations. Your help and understanding could be important in these situations.

In families where there is a mix of birth and adopted children, adopted children may feel that the birth child is the parents' favourite, so adopters may often have to walk on eggshells, managing the conflicting demands of the children.

Jealousy

Four-year-old Tyler was adopted into a family in which he had an older brother, Nathan, the birth child of the family. Tyler was convinced that Nathan had a bigger bedroom than he did – even after his parents measured it to prove to him that it was an identical size. The fact of the matter wasn't as important as his perception that Nathan had so many advantages because he had always lived in this family. That felt very unfair to Tyler, who had experienced abuse and neglect as a young child. His new parents understood this, and took whatever opportunities they found to reassure him how much he was loved and wanted. However, it was not until he was a much older teenager that he stopped feeling so jealous of his brother.

Conversely, how difficult must it be as a birth child if your parents have adopted a child who turns out to be cleverer, prettier or better at sport than you are? Of course, there are often differences of this kind between siblings who are born to their family, but there is an additional edge for the child whose parents have gone out and deliberately adopted – to a child, this can seem as if the parents were dissatisfied with them as their child. Again, being aware of children's feelings and making a conscious effort to reassure them of their place in their parents' affections is important.

Adopters are sometimes taken aback by the level of competitiveness between brothers and sisters and how fierce sibling rivalry can be. This is particularly the case if the adopters didn't have siblings themselves or if their experience of sibling relationships was generally harmonious. In such a situation, adopters may not know what would constitute a "normal" level of sibling rivalry for a family. But if they approach you for support, be careful not to dismiss their feelings by saying 'All children have arguments', even though this is largely true. This will simply make them feel that you haven't understood and that there is no point in talking to you about their problems.

It might be useful to suggest that they ask their friends who have children about the arguments their children have and how they manage them. Alternatively, you might be able to put them in touch with another adoptive family who have managed a similar problem so that they can gain comfort from knowing that their situation is not unique, and can share ideas for managing such behaviour.

Feeling guilty

If the adopter's birth child feels very jealous and competitive, the adopters may see a side of their existing child's behaviour and personality that they didn't know was there. This can be difficult and upsetting. They may start to wonder if they have done the right thing by adopting or if they have been unfair to their own child to put her in this situation.

Adoptive parents' feelings of guilt towards existing children of the family are known to be a factor in placement breakdown. Parents may reach a point where they feel it is not fair to expect their existing children to cope with the levels of stress in the family. In fact, social workers can also end up feeling guilty at times. 'If I'd known what it would have done to the family dynamics, I never would have placed this child into this family,' admitted one senior social worker. You should be aware that the adopters may experience these feelings, and be ready to discuss this with them.

Help from outside the family

Tell parents that when birth children are suffering, acknowledging their feelings and providing individual attention on a regular basis can help. For example, the child may have special time on her own after the adopted child has gone to bed, or it may be that on a Saturday, one parent spends time with the adopted child and the other has special time with the birth child. This can give each child the opportunity for individual attention. If there are more than two children in the family, this can be the time to involve a reliable granny or uncle in regularly taking a child out at the weekend so that all the children have some special time.

> *I fetched her from school on Thursdays and she came to my place. We made a ritual out of it...there was milk and a different cake I made for her every week.*
>
> *(Grandparent of an adopted ten-year-old girl, quoted in Argent, 2004, p 28)*

One family regularly employed a student to spend time at the weekend with one of the children to ensure that there was sufficient adult time for each of the children. This could be a suggestion if there is no available help within the adopters' family or support network, and might even involve the local authority in funding such a helper on the basis that this is a form of respite care within the family.

If the family is stressed and the problems seem hard to resolve, this would be an indicator that they might benefit from skilled professional help. Some local authorities employ a psychologist who has a brief to support adoptive families. Alternatively, you may refer the family to the local CAMHS. Hopefully, this specialist intervention will help the family members manage the stresses more successfully.

As parents, it is important to have a long-term view, and childhood difficulties often seem less important as the children mature. As children grow up into adulthood, jealousy often becomes less intense and people can appreciate the importance of the relationships they have with brothers and sisters, especially at times of family crisis. But – while it lasts – sibling rivalry can make for a stormy family life which tests both children and adults to the limit.

Key points

- Help family members to support the adopters by explaining that the adopted child will need time to learn the importance of their parents in their life, and about their place in their new family.
- Take time to meet with family members, if the adopters would like this, to talk about how they can help the new family.
- Discuss with adopters how the new child may impact on the other children in the family – this may include intense and unexpected sibling rivalry. Provide them with advice about how to manage this.
- If family relationships become difficult, acknowledge the adopters' feelings and possible guilt over this. Support – either from within the family or professional support – may be needed to help the family overcome these problems.

TIP 7

Help adopters to deal with contact

> *When it was time for one of those contact meetings, we always made a family occasion of it. We'd plan a picnic or some kind of outing and it would be the children and my daughter and son-in-law and me; Beryl (birth mother) would bring her mother along and that made it easier for the children...they could see that we all got on together.*
>
> (Grandparents of three, in Argent, 2004, p 35)

In many adoptions, some form of contact continues with the child's birth parents, birth siblings and/or other relatives. Contact is always a very sensitive area linking the two strands of the adopted child's heritage and needs careful planning on a case-by-case basis. It is important that social workers understand the level of anxiety that adopters may have about contact. Adopters are more likely to appreciate the need for contact if it is evident that arrangements are based on a good assessment of the child's lifelong needs.

Contact can take several different forms.

Letterbox contact

This is contact in the form of letters and photographs sent by the adoptive parents to the birth parent and/or birth family members. The adoption agency acts as the "letterbox" and preserves confidentiality about where the child lives.

Face-to-face contact with birth relatives

Face-to-face contact between an adopted child and one or more birth siblings happens quite frequently, and there may also be contact with other members of the extended family, such as with birth grandparents. In some situations, there may be a risk of a sibling or grandparent acting as a conduit for information from a hostile or distressed birth parent, and careful arrangements may be needed to monitor the situation and provide support to all parties.

In some cases, there can be benefits from contact between the child and the birth grandparents. However, some grandparents in this situation may have divided loyalties between their child (the birth mother or father) and their grandchild who has been adopted. In these situations it is important to be confident that the grandparent will prioritise the adopted child's right to protection and will not divulge any confidential information such as where they live. Where it works well, adoptive parents appreciate how important the contact is to their child and in some cases have invited the grandparents to increase their level of contact.

Face-to-face contact with birth parents

Face-to-face contact between a child who has been adopted and his birth parents is relatively unusual. It should happen only if the birth parents can be trusted not to undermine the child's relationship with the adoptive parents.

In many cases, those parents who have not been able to provide adequate care for their child are also unable to put his needs first by accepting the reality of the adoption and of their own changed role in their child's life. If they are vying for the child's affection or undermining the adopters, this places the child in a very invidious position.

In such a situation, contact will not help the child feel settled and secure, which is vital for a secure attachment to his adopters to develop – and which, in turn, is necessary for the child's healthy emotional development. However, in some situations direct contact with a birth parent is appropriate and important for a child's sense of identity. In these cases, it is important to match the child with adopters who understand and can support this contact. When children are excited before contact and remain pleased and happy about the opportunity to see a loved person from their past, it is important to support contact arrangements. When children are enjoying contact, adopters usually feel positive about it.

How are contact arrangements decided on?

There will be a contact plan with the care plan at the time a placement order (in England and Wales), permanence order (in Scotland) or freeing order (in Northern Ireland) is applied for. At this stage the adopters may not have been identified, and therefore their views on contact will not have been discussed.

Arrangements for contact can quite often become the subject of negotiation between the parties (i.e. the birth parents and the local authority) during the proceedings, which means that they may not represent a proposal based primarily on the child's needs. Once the order is made, and the child knows that he will not be returning home, the emphasis of work with him shifts. Over the course of time it may become clear that what was proposed at the stage of the court hearing is no longer entirely appropriate.

Contact plans need to be discussed with prospective adopters before the match goes to panel so that their views are represented. Plans are also reviewed at looked after children reviews, and at reviews of the adoptive placement, to ensure that they are still meeting the child's needs.

By the time the adoption application is made to the court, the plan for contact has often been modified. Courts are reluctant to make contact orders at the time of an adoption hearing, as that would limit the adopters' parental responsibility and their ability to change the contact arrangements if their child's needs alter over time, as is often the case. Adopters need to be able to make decisions about what is in their child's best interest. However, the report for the court will specify the proposed arrangements for contact on a voluntary basis and there is an expectation that these plans should be honoured unless the child's needs change.

All parties should be open to the possibility of contact arrangements changing and evolving over time. This should be included in the written agreement about contact which most local authorities draw up before the adoption is finalised. Some children might want less contact as they grow older, while others who did not have any contact initially may come to feel that it is important to them. If arrangements for contact are altered, the placing local authority would have a role in explaining and negotiating the proposed changes with the birth parents.

Circumstances and feelings can change for birth family members too, in which case they would usually discuss this, in the first instance, with the placing local authority.

The book *Ten Top Tips for Managing Contact* (Bond, 2007), provides more advice on managing contact arrangements.

Making letterbox contact work

Letterbox contact is sometimes assumed to be appropriate in all situations, but it has its own complexities and can present problems for some children. It should be based on the child's assessed needs, rather than devised in a "formulaic" manner.

If you are involved in making arrangements for contact, you might consider the following points.

- Letters should be exchanged between the birth parent and the adoptive parents rather than between the birth parent and the child. Experience teaches that birth parents' letters are often inappropriate and can be full of their own unhappiness which would be hard for the child to read. Work may need to be done with birth parents to help them consider the content of their letters to make this a more positive interaction for the child. If letters are addressed to the adopters, it is easier for them to consider whether it is appropriate to share the letters with the child, or to save them to share when the child is older.

- Adopters should let their child know that they write to their birth mother, or siblings, or grandparents once or twice a year to let them know how the child is doing. It can store up problems if the child feels something has been done behind his back. Some children like to enclose a drawing or choose a photo to enclose with the letter; others are happy for their mother or father to do this. Over time, children may come to have a different view of contact, which will need to be taken into account.

- In some cases, there is one-way letterbox contact – from the adopters to the birth parents, but not vice versa. This may be appropriate if the birth parents are very antagonistic or unrealistic about the adoption and it can be anticipated that their letters would be undermining or attacking.

- Most adopters feel that it is a reasonable expectation to write to birth parents at least once a year, both in order to provide them with information, but also as a means of keeping a thread of communication open. It can be helpful in future years if their child wants to make contact with his birth parent if the adopter has written regularly. This can enable the adopter to have a role in setting up any contact.

- There can be an assumption by the social workers that it is reassuring for the birth parents to hear about the child and what is going on in his life. However, this may not be true if the child is going through a "bad patch", for example, truanting from school or in trouble with the police. Adopters may also feel that they do not want to share such information with the birth parent, as it is their child's private information, so that writing letters can become a minefield.

- Everyone involved must be sensitive to the child's needs, and for some children the thought of any contact with abusive parents is intolerable.

One nine-year-old boy was terrified that the letterbox contact would make it possible for his mother to trace him despite all the reassurances he was given. Eventually the contact was stopped, even though his adopters felt very guilty that they were reneging on their promise to his birth mother.

- For some children, contact from their birth parents can be re-traumatising. If, for instance, a birth mother is mentally ill and suffering delusions, clearly she cannot be held responsible for her mental illness – but this does not mean it is in the child's best interests to have letters from her. For the child, hearing from their mother again could be frightening and could bring back very scary memories. Similarly, a child who has suffered abuse may well have flashbacks if there is any form of contact. As social workers, we cannot always anticipate which children will have such reactions, but if adopters say that their child is affected, you need to take what they say seriously and review the arrangements with the adopters.
- In many cases birth parents stop collecting letters – they may have transient and chaotic lifestyles and sometimes letters sit in a file, unopened, for years. Adopters may feel uneasy to think that they are writing "into a void", and some prefer to stop writing for a while, until the birth parent is in touch with the local authority again.

AN EXTRA SET OF GRANDPARENTS

Sally had a serious mental health breakdown and her daughter Lauren was eventually adopted when she was three. There is no contact between Sally and Lauren.

Sally's parents, Amy and Philip, are very involved in supporting their daughter. They were also keen not to lose touch with their granddaughter. They fully understood why Sally was not allowed contact and they undertook to protect the adoptive family's confidentiality. The adoptive parents agreed that it would be good for Lauren to maintain her relationship with her grandparents.

Twice a year, Amy and Philip visit Lauren and her adoptive family. They bring presents for all the children in the family, not just Lauren. Lauren is happy about it and the family sees them almost as an extra set of grandparents.

Amy and Philip are also able to let Sally know that Lauren is well loved and thriving, and despite the sadness of their situation, they feel relieved that they have been able to maintain some link with Lauren. When Lauren is older and wants to know more about Sally, the link with her grandparents will be helpful.

Contact between siblings

Generally, it is assumed that siblings should, if possible, be adopted by the same family. This ensures an ongoing relationship with someone to whom they are related by birth, and helps them develop a positive identity as they grow up.

However, sometimes this is not possible: siblings may have very different needs which would be difficult to manage within one family. For example, a child may be adopted, and then some years later a sibling may come into care and need to be adopted, but the adopted child may be having difficulties, and the adopters may need to concentrate their efforts on helping her, rather than introducing another child into the family.

An adopted child may have contact with:

- siblings who were adopted (or in a long-term foster placement) by another family – possibly in the past, or at a later stage when another child from the same birth family needs to be adopted;
- a sibling adopted at the same time into a different family, where the two adoptive families decide to keep in touch with each other;
- older children who have remained with their birth parent or another member of the extended family.

The frequency of contact varies. For school-age children, it might take place during school holidays.

CONTACT WITH AN OLDER SISTER

When Delia was adopted at the age of eight, she had a teenage sister who was living in a long-term foster family but still in contact with her mother. Delia's adopters agreed to support ongoing contact between Delia and her sister. Every school holiday, the children spent some time together.

Ten years on, they have maintained the regular contact and the relationship they have is important to them both. Because the older sister is in touch with her birth mother, Delia made contact with her sooner than would otherwise have been the case.

Fortunately, Delia has a very close and stable relationship with her adopters, who feel very confident in their role as her parents. They have been able to talk to her about her confused feelings and to help her find a way to manage the conflicts of loyalty that sometimes arise when her birth mother says things about her adoptive parents that are undermining.

Most adopters are quick to appreciate how special it would be for their child to grow up knowing someone to whom he is related by birth. If siblings have been adopted by different families, it is generally possible to arrange some form of ongoing contact. Giving the two sets of adopters the opportunity to meet as adults first, to break the ice and discuss what might work for their children, enables the adopters to feel ownership of the plan. This makes it more likely that the contact will work well and continue.

However, you cannot legislate for "chemistry" between people, and sometimes the two families do not find that they have much in common. Contact of this kind is sometimes a pleasure and sometimes a duty – but even if it seems onerous, families will usually make the effort if they can see how important it is for their child to have contact with a brother or sister.

As a social worker you need to bear in mind that, for the adoptive family, arranging contact with several birth siblings and possibly other members of the extended family – and ensuring that there is still some space for an active social life – could prove difficult. There needs to be some sense of what is reasonable and achievable for the family, and geography and other logistical considerations will come into play in deciding this.

Potential problems with sibling contact

- Sometimes plans for the siblings do not work out. If one sibling's adoption disrupts, there is a risk that the other child's sense of security could be threatened by the knowledge of what has happened to his brother or sister. In addition, if the child whose adoption disrupted subsequently has contact with the birth parent/s, future contact between the siblings can become a vehicle for the birth parent to send messages to the adopted child.

- In some cases, children and young people develop a strong desire to see their younger siblings who were adopted into a different family. However, sometimes what is in one child's best interests is not in the other child's interests. This is particularly true if the older sibling is very troubled, for example, or is in trouble with the police or using drugs. In this case, the adoptive parents of the younger sibling may understandably wish to protect their child from the stress of worrying about their older sibling – or of being tempted to emulate their lifestyle.

- Different children have different needs and this is true of siblings too, particularly as they may have had different experiences. One child may have been scapegoated by his parents or bullied by the sibling who now wants contact, and the two children's memories of family life may be at odds. So it can sometimes happen that one child's social worker (or adopter) may feel it is in the child's interests to maintain contact with a brother or sister – but that the other child's social worker (or the adopter) may have a different view about the benefits of contact for the child she is responsible for. Sadly, the needs of siblings are sometimes incompatible, which is very painful for the adults as well as for the child, who may feel rejected and bereft.

- Be aware of the possibility that feelings about past abuse (actual or suspected) might be stirred up by contact. For a child who has been abused, even seeing a sibling who was also being abused, or who may have been an abuser himself, can bring the trauma back to mind. Some children cannot bear to see anyone who was associated with that part of their lives for many years. Again, this can be extremely painful for the child who wants contact, but if seeing his sibling re-traumatises the other child, that would be unacceptable. Letterbox contact may be a more acceptable alternative in such situations.

Contact with siblings is often a real bonus for adopted children as a means of preserving a positive relationship from their past, but it is important to consider the balance of risks and benefits in each individual case.

Teenagers

Sometimes sibling contact may be constructive while the children are younger. However, problems can arise if the older sibling begins "acting out", for example, by using drugs, or if he has made contact with potentially abusive birth parents. Adopters may wish to protect their child under such circumstances.

However, there may come a point at which a teenager takes matters into his own hands by trying to trace his siblings (if he does not have their contact details already) or to get in touch with his birth parents.

Lucy, aged 14, traced her older sisters through the networking site Facebook with no difficulty. They were initially welcoming of her. However, they had their own problems and did not in reality have much time for a little sister, so the contact rather fizzled out. This was a disappointment to Lucy, but less of a problem than if the older siblings had tried to involve her in some of their troubled relationships.

In this age of electronic communications, there are real issues about young people potentially tracing (or being traced by) someone from their past. Although this may, to some extent, be outside the control of the adults, it is nevertheless important not to abdicate responsibility.

The adopters must do what they can as protective parents to ensure they know who their child is seeing and where they go, and talk to their child about the possible dangers of social networking sites like Facebook, and of giving information about themselves to people via the internet. As a social worker, it is important that you can provide advice about how adopters can manage such situations.

The older the young person is, the more their views will be taken into account in deciding about contact, as about other matters. Once an adopted person turns 18, he has the right to approach the local authority or adoption support agency for themselves to ask for help in tracing or contacting their birth family.

Most social workers would encourage the young person to involve their adopters in such discussions as, at 18, many young people are still somewhat impulsive and may not really think through the implications of their actions. If he does contact his birth family, he is likely to need a great deal of support while he makes sense of whatever relationship develops. He may also face the trauma of rejection, or of discovering that his birth parents' lives are unhappy or chaotic, which could be distressing for him.

When birth parents try to trace children

Adoptions are generally arranged so as to protect the adoptive family's confidentiality, and most birth parents understand that, although it is painful for them, they cannot have contact with their child other than via agreed contact arrangements. If a birth parent is seeking information about their child, he or she will usually contact the local authority, and the social worker may then speak to the adopters to discuss the contact with them and seek their views about what information can be shared. You may be involved in such discussions.

However, there are a small number of parents whose children have been adopted who will go to great lengths to track down their children. In the present day, with the possibilities presented by the internet, this is becoming harder to control.

- Many children and young people have a profile on a social networking site, such as Facebook, often giving personal details. Adopters should talk to their children about the benefits and risks of

this and should, as far as possible, monitor their use of the internet.
- If there is letterbox contact, the adoptive parents should be careful not to inadvertently provide any details about the child or their home which could give away their location.
- Photographs are often a treasured part of letterbox contact for birth parents. In a few rare cases, however, photographs sent as part of letterbox contact have been used to trace a child, for example, sending photographs in which the child appears in his school uniform could be a way for a determined birth parent to track down a child. All identifying features should be removed.

A birth father who had been sent a copy of the child's official school photograph found the telephone number of the photographer's studio on the back and managed to persuade someone there into disclosing the child's address.

- There have also been isolated examples of a birth parent posting a photo of their child (which they received via letterbox contact) on the internet with a story that they have lost touch with their child because of a family dispute, and asking for help to find them. This has resulted in a child's whereabouts being divulged by someone who had no idea of the consequences. Such cases, although uncommon as yet, point to the need for caution about including photos in letterbox arrangements if there are serious concerns about how someone in the birth family network might use them.

Sharing information about the birth family with a child

A difficult issue for adopters is deciding what to do when they receive some potentially upsetting news from their adopted child's birth family. For instance, learning that his birth mother has had another baby could be quite upsetting for the child. If he himself was neglected or abused, he might be anxious about another baby being in the same situation. On the other hand, if his parents are able to care for their new child, what does it feel like to be the child they abused or rejected? The adopters are the people who know their child best, and they should be the ones to make the decisions about when and how to convey such information, but your advice may be of great help to them.

- Adopters should not feel obliged to tell the child any information straight away. They need to reflect on the possible impact on their child and to find the most constructive way to share the information.
- If there is a plan for a younger sibling of the child to be adopted, adopters might want to wait until a family has been identified, so that they have something reassuring to tell their child – and possibly, by that stage, they could be thinking of a meeting with the younger sibling. In some situations, adopters will decide to wait until the subject comes up naturally and perhaps the child asks for more information. For example, adopted children do sometimes wonder whether their birth parent has had another child. If this comes up, the adopter could offer to find out some more, and then share the information carefully.
- Adopters have a duty to be protective of their child and to consider his best interests. They need to remember that it would be better for their child to hear such information from themselves than for it to come as a shock if their child has future contact with his birth family.

In considering sensitive issues such as contact, adoption social workers should bear in mind that the primary school years are a time of upset and disturbance for many adopted children. Generally, the under-fives accept what they are told without too much questioning. The story of being adopted and "chosen" can seem like a fairy story with a happy ending. Children of primary school age, on the other hand, are able to conceptualise more, and they may begin to wonder, worry and raise questions about why they were adopted and why their birth mother or father couldn't care for them. Children of this age need answers which address some of these difficulties in language they can understand. It is important to be truthful about difficulties in their birth family, as without understanding the real reason for their adoption, some children idealise their birth parents and blame their adopters. This reinforces the dynamic of rejecting the new family, and can make it impossible for the child to allow the adopters to offer nurturing care. Truthful information should be geared to the child's developmental stage and should not be overwhelming. However, helping a child understand their upset feelings and where they come from is much better than trying to pretend that nothing bad happened.

These kinds of conversations may be useful for you to role-play with the adopters, or they may find it useful for you to give them suggestions of age-appropriate ways to explain events in their child's past. For example, instead of simply saying 'Your mum was too young and she didn't know how to look after you', the adopter might now say something like 'Your mum was young, and she didn't understand that babies need to have their feeds very regularly or they get too hungry. You were often hungry and also cold because your mum didn't wrap you up warmly when she took you out. All babies need to be cared for so they feel safe. The social worker tried to help your mum learn how to care for you. But when this didn't work, the social worker asked the wise judge what the best plan for you would be. The wise judge said that you were a little baby who needed a mum (and dad) who could look after you and keep you safe till you were grown up. He decided that you should be adopted by your own special mum and/or dad.' Some time later, the story might be elaborated to include information that their child's birth mother grew up in care and did not have a mother to care for her when she was little.

Another scenario could be: Your birth mother often felt unhappy and one day someone gave her some drugs to make her feel better. The trouble with drugs is that they only make you feel better for a short time, so soon your birth mother felt unhappy again and had to find some more drugs. Soon she was spending all her money on them, and she still felt miserable. She didn't have the money to buy you the right baby food or to keep the flat warm. Babies need to be safe and well cared for, and if their parents can't look after them, they need to be with a family who can give them the care they need.'

It is helpful for you, as the social worker, to think about how best to explain such stories to the child and to ensure that what is in the child's life story book explains their history honestly. It is important that you take responsibility for giving the child this information, together with the adopters. They will then be able to reiterate this information in later years.

This might be a good time to revisit the child's life story book. Often it is best for the child to do such a piece of work with the adopters, who will have a sense of what he needs to know. Joy Rees has written a very helpful book: *Life Story Books: A family-friendly approach* (2009), which gives valuable advice on presenting the child's story in a way which reinforces the idea that he has now found a safe and secure family to love him, as well as finding constructive ways to talk about the sad and difficult things that have happened. There are a number of other books available on this subject.

Although there may be times when contact is not manageable for a child, it is important that the adopters always maintain what Brodzinsky refers to as communicative openness, i.e. the willingness to help the child to think about his story and to answer his questions (whether they are voiced or implied) honestly. Whether or not the child is having contact, it should be made clear that adoption and the child's birth family are safe subjects that can be openly discussed in the adoptive family.

Sadness and separation

Adoption does, of course, involve feelings of loss and separation for the children involved, as well as for the adults, and social workers should try to help children deal with these feelings. It is sometimes assumed that if a child has contact with birth family members, he will not feel so sad, as if that will wipe out the loss. However, in practice, contact can be stressful for children and may simply serve to reinforce the feelings of loss and guilt that so many children feel when they become looked after.

The benefits of contact may outweigh the potential difficulties. However, social workers need to recognise that contact inevitably involves feelings of sadness for the child, his birth relatives and perhaps his adoptive parents too.

If contact seems to be preventing the child from moving on, and causing difficulties that do not seem to be lessening over time, you may need to consider whether it should continue at this stage in the child's life. Occasionally, a break in contact may be beneficial for the child, and it should not be assumed that this is a failure, or that contact has to be stopped for good.

It is important to remember that contact issues do not have to be resolved within a few months or years. Adopted children sometimes need to devote their energies to learning how to be a child and to trust the new parents in their lives, to making friends and learning at school. They may not have the ability to manage contact if it reawakens complex feelings. But this does not mean that the time will not come, perhaps when they are young adults, when they feel ready to make more sense of their birth family history and perhaps to contact someone from the past. Indeed, it is often when adopted people have grown up and established themselves that they can manage the complexities of dealing with the conflicts of loyalty and the sadness of recognising the difficulties their birth parents faced.

If their adopters have maintained letterbox contact with their birth parents, that can help open the door. If the adopters have maintained an open dialogue with their child about her history over the years, he will be better prepared, and will hopefully feel confident that his adopters will be there to support him during this important stage of the lifelong adoption journey.

Eve had been adopted at the age of four. Her birth mother had mental health difficulties, and Eve experienced many changes of carer before she came into care. Eve's adolescence was quite troubled and she contacted her local authority several times to ask for help in tracing her birth mother, both when she was in her teens and later when she was living away from her adopters at the age of 22. However, she never followed these requests through.

By the age of 33, Eve had married and had a baby daughter. She felt settled and secure emotionally, and at this stage she once again approached her local authority to put her in touch with her birth mother, Shelley. This time she followed through, and eventually she had a reunion which was inevitably very emotional. Shelley was thrilled to see Eve and also to meet the baby. However, Shelley remained a very vulnerable and needy woman; Eve was able to work out a pattern of contact with Shelley that enabled her to keep in touch, but did not result in Shelley taking over the family's life with all her own problems and difficulties. Eve later commented that it had been extremely important to her to re-establish a relationship with Shelley, but that she would have been completely overwhelmed by Shelley's needs if she had made contact before she had matured and found her feet as an adult.

Key points

- Ensure that plans for contact are settled for the child in a timely and appropriate manner, and that the child's needs are fully taken into account.
- Contact may need to change over time. Be available to discuss this with the adopters.
- Contact, even letterbox contact, may not run smoothly. Be aware of this and ensure that the adopters are aware of this possibility too, and be available to discuss the situation and work out strategies if necessary.
- Many things should be considered when working out contact plans and, particularly if the adopted child has siblings, there may be many views to take into account. Be aware that sometimes the best solution will be a compromise between the needs of the different children and adults involved.
- Ensure that the adopters realise that care should be taken when sharing contact information with their child. Even minor details can have great significance for the child.
- Conversely, care should be taken by the adopters when sharing contact information with the birth parents/relatives. The child's safety and wellbeing must be the foremost consideration.

TIP 8

Provide different kinds of support to meet individual families' needs

We couldn't have done without all the help the agency gave us right up to the time she was 18. And then they kept in touch and helped out when we had problems with benefits and wheelchairs and things because they knew her, and the adult disability team in our area didn't understand about adoption.

(Adopter of young person with multiple impairments, in Argent, 2004, p19)

There are many reasons why a child or family may have particular needs for support. Whatever these are, you are likely to have to involve other professionals and local services in order to arrange appropriate support for the family. It is helpful to develop a network of local contacts who can advise or support the adopters on issues to do with, for instance, health or education.

Health, including emotional and behavioural difficulties

The local authority placing the child will contact the family's GP, enclosing the child's adoption medical at the time of placement. The child will continue to have looked-after medicals from the GP or community paediatrician until the adoption order is made. The health visitor from the placing authority should similarly be asked to send their notes to the child's new health visitor. The adopters should also be given the child's health record of immunisations, etc, at the time of placement.

If the child has emotional/behavioural problems, she may be referred to the local Child And Adolescent Mental Health Service (CAMHS). However, provision across the UK is patchy and some CAMHS services may not have adoption experience or expertise. In these situations, you may need to liaise with the clinic to ensure that the impact of the child's early experience of adversity on her current behaviour is understood. Where adopters have the experience of being treated as if they had caused the child's difficulties, because their local clinic has not had experience of adoption, this is very unhelpful to new parents who are stressed and are indeed doing their best to compensate for the child's earlier traumatic experiences.

An increasing number of local authorities have appointed a child psychologist, child psychotherapist or family therapist who specialises in adoption issues, as part of their post-adoption team. This may be a joint appointment with the local CAMHS. This person can be helpful not only in identifying and addressing a child's problems, but also in engaging with the CAMHS in another local authority, if the child is being adopted in a different area. If no such link already exists, the local authority's post-adoption service might discuss ways of accessing such support with the local CAMHS.

Adopters may need help in making the initial referral or need ongoing support from their social worker, e.g. in liaison meetings with CAMHS where a therapeutic intervention is offered. Although the family GP can refer a child to CAMHS, he or she will not have access to the record of the child's early experiences. It is very helpful if the social worker can provide a summary of the relevant issues at the time of referral to CAMHS.

Education

Many children placed for adoption struggle to cope with the demands of the classroom. They are often emotionally immature, and not ready to manage group situations where they need to co-operate and wait their turn along with a large group of other children. They can find it hard to concentrate and are often disruptive, causing stress to the teacher and the rest of the class. Arranging for them to have appropriate support in the classroom is a priority.

Some local authorities have an educational psychologist for looked after children, and all local education authorities have a duty to prioritise meeting the needs of looked after children. However, the same priority is not given to meeting the needs of children once they are adopted, which means it is particularly important to ensure that children's needs are assessed and appropriate plans put in place to support them before the adoption order is granted.

If the child has identified special educational needs, she may have been assessed by the educational psychologist before placement, who should then liaise with their opposite number in the receiving local authority once placement is decided upon. In most cases, children with special educational needs will attend mainstream schools with additional support and it is important that liaison takes place with the new school at an early stage. All looked after children of school age have a Personal Education Plan (PEP) (Personal Learning Plan (PLP) in Scotland), which records and updates their progress and sets targets. The PEP is reviewed periodically. Those children who have been identified as having some additional needs will be on "school action" or "school action plus", to ensure that their needs are being met. These children will have an Individual Education Plan (IEP) (Individual Education Programme in Scotland), which sets targets and identifies resources. The IEP is also reviewed periodically.

Schools must also ensure that children with a high level of educational needs are also provided for. The terminology surrounding such provision differs between countries within the UK, but the outcome for children should be similar. In England and Wales, children may be assessed for a Statement of Educational Needs. Schools have a Special Educational Needs Co-ordinator (SENCO) who is often the best point of contact to discuss what support a child will need. Schools have a modest budget of their own to provide support for identified children. However, a number of adopted children need a substantial amount of support to manage in the classroom because of their emotional needs. Alternatively, for some children the problem may be that they cannot cope with unstructured time in the playground and may need support at those times. Where additional support is needed, which the school cannot fund from its own budget, there needs to be consideration of whether this can be provided for as part of the adoption support package from the placing local authority. Your local authority may have an education worker responsible for looked after children.

Many school-age adopted children struggle in the classroom and getting proper support for them in school is a significant task for the social workers involved. Schools often do not understand the issues that affect adopted children, and may see them simply as "problem" children who are being "naughty". This is particularly the case where the teacher is not aware of the child's history and adoptive status – without this knowledge it may be difficult for the teacher to make sense of why the child is presenting so many problems. You should discuss with the adopters how best to approach the school and what the school should be told of their child's past difficulties. It is important to remember that the adopters are the parents, and their views should be respected. They may be reluctant to "label" their child, and there is a balance to be struck between respecting the confidentiality of the child's personal story and giving the school staff the information they need in order to understand the child. It may be helpful to discuss with a key person, e.g. the head teacher, SENCO, etc, whether and how much individual teachers need to know about the child's history.

If there are continuing difficulties with the child at school, it is often helpful to arrange a meeting between the adopters and the child's teacher and the SENCO, or whoever else is involved, to discuss the situation. It is often very reassuring for a troubled child to know that the adults are in communication and are working together to find a way to help her with her difficulties. Regular communication, including termly meetings, is often a positive strategy to provide support to the school and to the adopters in managing a child with challenging behaviour. Adopters may want you to be involved in these meetings.

If the child has a particularly high need for support because of a disability or emotional needs, this support may be appropriately funded in England and Wales via a Statement of Special Educational Needs, or similar provision in Scotland, e.g. a Co-ordinated Support Plan. You should support the parents through the process and liaise with the school. The educational psychologist would be a key figure in assessing the child's needs, and good communication with them is essential. (See Tip 10 for other sources of support.) In recent times, more of the budget for supporting children with special needs in the classroom has been devolved to schools, and a relatively small budget is held centrally by the local education authority (LEA). In order to access funding from the LEA in England and Wales, it is important that the Statement of Educational Needs indicates that the child's needs can be described as "low incidence" needs. Problems which are often experienced by a number of other children (high incidence needs) should be funded by the school. The LEA only funds resources to meet more unusual "low incidence" needs, for example, an adopted child who has experienced many moves and rejection in the past may react extremely badly to unexpected changes such as a supply teacher replacing their favourite teacher, or even to changes in routine such as altered play times. Such a child may need one to one support at key times, and if this can be shown to be an unusual ("low incidence") requirement, which is not a common problem, the support can be funded by the LEA. The social worker will be asked to provide a report to support the application for a Statement of Educational Needs, and this is the opportunity to explain the relevant early history of the child and its impact on the child's current difficulties in the classroom.

Children with a disability

> *We continued to have regular co-ordination*
> *meetings after William moved in with us. The*
> *purpose of these was to see to practical matters,*
> *ensure all the therapeutic arrangements were in*
> *hand, and to look at contact issues. These meetings*
> *were generally attended by William's social worker*
> *and her senior, our social worker, and, at first, his*
> *previous foster carer, Janet.*
>
> (Marsden, 2008, p 39)

Families which adopt a child who has a disability often have some previous experience of disability, so this is a positive choice for them. They are able to see the child first and foremost, with their individual wishes, feelings and needs, and with the added challenge of having an impairment.

Before the match is agreed, the adopters should have the opportunity to meet with the relevant community paediatrician, specialists and therapists closely involved with the child's care. It is good practice for the medical adviser to share all appropriate information with the prospective adopters, and to discuss the needs of the child with whom they are matched. It is also good practice to provide a written report of this meeting. At the time of placement, it would be helpful to agree whether the medical adviser or the disability consultant will arrange a referral to appropriate services in the new area. Adopters of children with disabilities or other special needs must be prepared to be advocates for their children to ensure they receive appropriate services, and they may need your support in trying to access resources at times.

Children with disabilities may be entitled to Disability Living Allowance and if they are not already receiving this, applying for it should be considered. Adopters of children with disabilities also need to ensure that they are claiming any other state benefits they are entitled to (see Tip 9). They may also be entitled to apply to the local authority for financial support to meet the adopted child's needs (again, see Tip 9). You should ensure that the adopters are aware of all these possibilities for financial support.

If a service the child needs is not available without a long wait, it may be appropriate to consider whether the local authority could fund an assessment and some short-term support privately. Often children placed for adoption have repeatedly missed out on receiving the specialist services they need. This may be because their birth family was not able to keep hospital appointments or to implement advice from therapists, or because the child has been moved between foster homes, and therefore never reached the top of the waiting list. Whatever the reason, it may well be that the adopted child has already suffered multiple delays in addition to her disability, and every effort should be made to support the adopters in accessing the services their child needs without further delay.

Families who have children with disabilities may need to be offered respite care by local authorities, to enable them to have regular day or weekend breaks from their caring responsibilities. This should be identified in the adoption support plan, either for current or future resourcing. Bear in mind that the family may need your help in making this referral. Adoptive families are often less likely to use respite care, perhaps because as adopters they are keen to care for their child at home, and reluctant for her to go back into what they might regard as "care". In addition, the child will need a period of settled life in her new family in order to build attachments and to believe that this is a "forever" family. Consequently, it may be several months or even years before some families request respite care. For some families and children, a regular babysitter to allow the family time to attend special events with other siblings, or for the adults to have some "me-time" would be more appropriate than, for instance, a weekend break. Respite care should be presented in a flexible and creative way which encourages the adopters to think about what would give them and their family the best opportunity for everyone to benefit from this kind of support, and may include involvement from their own support network of family or friends.

Sadly, many parents who have a child with a disability say the hardest part is battling with officialdom and bureaucracy to get the services their child needs, and resilience and persistence are important qualities for any parent of a child with disabilities. Adoptive parents of children with disabilities have to contend with the same frustrations and delays in obtaining many of the things that their child needs, whether it is a new wheelchair or a Statement of Special Educational Needs. Both you, as the social worker, and the adopters will need to develop skills of advocacy and assertiveness.

National self-help groups for families who have children with a particular disability are an important source of support for adopters of children with disabilities. These organisations can often put parents in touch with other local families with children who have similar impairments.

- The national charity Contact a Family (see Tip 10) may be able to help if you have difficulty finding a support group for a particular disability or condition. Their website lists national support organisations for a wide range of conditions and disabilities.
- Contact a Family also has a database of local support groups for families who have a child with any disability.
- Contact a Family can also make links, on a one-to-one basis, between families of children with rare conditions for which there is no support group.
- Support groups often have websites, a message board or social networking site – check the internet for local groups.

Lesbian and gay adoptive parents

[The local authority] run a support group for adopters, which is about every couple of months. We helped them set up a gay and lesbian support group, which is open to any gay adopters or prospective adopters in the North East of England.

(Suzie and Jane, in Hill, 2009, p 161)

Gay and lesbian adopters face the same issues as other adopters, but in addition, they face the stigma that still exists in some parts of society towards gay men and lesbians as parents. Discussing possible problems and situations with them before they occur can help them to be more prepared to deal with future difficulties.

It is especially important for these adopters, given the prejudice in some quarters, that they are warmly supported by their network, either family and/or close friends. Preparing their families and friends for their adoption plans is an important aspect of the preparation process. Some applicants wait until their plans are reasonably well advanced before broaching the subject with some of their relatives. However, they do need to reach a point where they feel confident that those people who are important to them, and who will remain part of their lives once their child is placed, will support the adoption and give their child positive messages.

Gay or lesbian adoptive parents also need to prepare for the likelihood that their adopted child may face teasing and name-calling at times, and to think of strategies to support her. Although this is in some ways similar to what children born to same-sex couples experience, it does make a difference if you are born into a family and grow up always accepting the relationships between the adults. Especially for those children who are already of school age, being placed with lesbian or gay parents can raise awkward issues. However, if the adopters are introduced to their child in a straightforward, positive way by the social worker, and if the child observes that the foster carers and other adults who meet the adopters have confidence in them, this will help her to make a relationship with her new parents.

The adoptive parents may need help to deal with prejudice from outside the family as well. Choosing a school is important, and the adopters need to find a school they feel comfortable with – they should meet the head teacher and ask about the school's approach to issues such as diversity, bullying and teaching children about family life. Even if these issues have been covered at the time of placement, they can recur again later in a child's school life, perhaps when moving to a new school or as they grow older.

The child may also have to deal with her own complicated feelings as she struggles to fit in with new classmates who, sooner or later, may go through a phase of expressing anti-gay sentiments. This is a common pattern in the playground from time to time, and whilst the school may have very good anti-bullying and anti-homophobic policies, nevertheless, for a newly adopted child who is not very secure about her identity, this kind of name-calling can present a real challenge.

Some children are able to share their upset with their teacher or their parent if there has been name-calling or bullying. The adoptive parents should discuss such an incident with the school if their child tells them of such an experience. If the school has been alerted to the problem, staff members will often respond by putting in place some teaching about different kinds of families, and reminding all the children that name-calling is not allowed. This is often sufficient to deal with the problem, but in some cases the adopters may need to be assertive to ensure that the school responds effectively if their child is being bullied, and may need social work support to do this.

Some children with low self-esteem who are desperate to fit in with their new classmates might join in with name-calling, and some adopted children have come home and repeated these remarks to their gay or lesbian adopters. This can feel devastating to the adopters; however, it is important to help them remember that the child will have no real concept of same-sex relationships. It is important for the adopters not to react punitively. All children are quick to learn if something upsets their parents, and it would not be helpful for this to become a "weapon" for the child to use to attack the adopters with when she is upset or angry. A better approach would be to suggest that the adopters discuss in quite a low-key way the fact that there are different kinds of families, and as long as people love each other and look after each other, that is what is important. It is, of course, also important for the adopters to be clear about the kind of language that is hurtful, and not allowed in their family. Books which discuss different kinds of families can be a good way of opening up a discussion with a child – BAAF has published several children's books which cover this subject, along with *The Pink Guide to Adoption for Lesbians and Gay Men* (Hill, 2009), which discusses some of the specific issues that lesbians and gay men may encounter during the adoption process.

EXPLAINING TO FRIENDS

Richard and Tony adopted seven-year-old Peter and were keen to help him make friends. Peter invited a new school friend, Andrew, home for tea. Richard saw Andrew's mother in the playground and told her the address and arranged the time, but before he could say anything else, they were interrupted by the boys coming out of school.

Peter and Andrew had a good time playing together. But when Andrew's father arrived in the evening to collect him, Andrew asked him: 'Richard is Peter's daddy – so is Tony his uncle?' Richard and Tony held their breath as they waited to see how Andrew's father would respond to his son. Fortunately, Andrew's father had accurately summed up the situation. He rose to the occasion and gave a simple but warm explanation of how there are all kinds of families in the world and some children, like Peter, have two daddies.

Richard and Tony heaved a sigh of relief – and resolved that next time Peter wanted to have a friend home to play, they would make sure they had a quiet chat with the parents beforehand.

Gay and lesbian parents might appreciate the opportunity to share their experiences with other gay and lesbian adopters, and could make links through self-help organisations (see later in this book for useful organisations).

Black and minority ethnic adopters

Black and minority ethnic adopters – and those in mixed ethnicity relationships – face the same issues as other adopters, but also need to be aware that their children are likely to experience racism at some stage. Preparing their children for such experiences and building a positive identity is an important aspect of their parenting task. For the child who is adopted within a family which shares a similar ethnic background to their own, this can happen in a natural way. It is important, however, for adopters to also support their child at school and in the wider community. The choice of school will be important, and black and minority ethnic adopters will want to visit the school and reassure themselves about its attitude to diversity and, in particular, to racism.

You should be sensitive to the dimension of ethnicity when working with black and minority ethnic adoptive families. However, it is important not to treat families as if they all belong to one community and share the same issues. Different families will have many individual differences, and their particular ethnic background and their own experiences of living in the UK, and how they deal with racism will vary. It is important to take the time to get to know each family, and to discover what issues you can help them with.

Adopters often particularly value support from other adopters in a similar situation, and some agencies run support groups for black adopters which might be a helpful resource for some families. In areas where there are no such support groups, social workers may be able to put black and minority ethnic adopters in touch with others to provide support.

In addition to all the other tasks facing them as adoptive parents, black and minority ethnic parents must help their child to be proud of her ethnic identity and heritage. In some cases this can be complicated, if the child sees her adverse experiences with her birth parents as somehow connected with her and their ethnicity. However, over time, the experience of living with parents who share her ethnic background, but who are reliable and caring, should provide a reparative experience.

Children of mixed heritage are likely to have particular identity issues, and one of the ways you can support the adopters in opening up a discussion about the child's background is via the child's life story book, which could devote a section to giving some information and photos about the cultures and countries where the child's birth family originated.

In areas where there is an ethnically mixed population (which includes much of urban UK), it is important that the local authority social work staff group reflects this, so that adopters approaching the local authority/agency for support can see that the agency is reflective of diversity. In agencies where there are only a few black or minority ethnic adoptive parents, it is helpful to encourage adopters to bring a friend or relative with them to workshops or other meetings if they would like to do so, to ensure they do not feel isolated if there are no other black families present.

Transracial placements and overseas adoptions

White adoptive parents who have a black or mixed heritage child placed with them will have particular issues where they are likely to need support. It can be an unpleasant shock if they suddenly meet with racist comments and attitudes they may have never encountered before, including intrusive questions about their child's parentage. It is always deeply upsetting to be on the receiving end of racist comments, but for a transracial adopter, such an attack can also undermine their confidence as parents to their child. Preparing adopters before a child is placed forewarns them, but if and when they have such an experience, they will need to share it with someone and discuss strategies and ways of protecting their child. It is important that you are available to provide such support, if required.

Families who adopt a child from overseas may have similar experiences if visible differences between them and their child arouse people's curiosity. Finding ways to deflect unwanted curiosity and to reinforce their role as parents is an important aspect of claiming their child. Again, you should offer advice and support if needed.

Although there are undoubtedly complexities involved in adopting children from overseas, and in transracial adoptions, nevertheless, there are children for whom the decision has been taken that this is their best chance of enjoying the stability and care of growing up in a family. Once the decision has been made and the child is in placement, it is essential that professionals are positive and supportive towards the new parents. The adopters are the child's parents, and as such they need as much support as possible to enable them to meet their child's particular needs.

Like any other adoptive parents, those who adopt transracially need to find ways to help their child develop a positive sense of identity – which includes her ethnic heritage and culture. You can help by suggesting ways in which they can do this.

● Research shows that it is very important for children to attend schools where there is a good ethnic mix of children and staff. This ensures that they do not feel isolated, and that there are adult role models for them to identify with.

● When inviting children from school to visit their home, parents of black and minority ethnic children should make an effort to encourage friendships with other children from the same or a similar ethnic background. This might also give the opportunity to develop a friendship with the other children's parents.

● The adoptive parents could seek out other networks such as scouts, sports clubs and community groups where there are people of the same ethnic background who can be positive role models for their child.

● The family could attend events which celebrate the culture and traditions of the child's country of origin.

● The family could make a point of sitting down together to watch television programmes that are relevant to the child's background.

● When the adopters' child is old enough, they could introduce her to literature that will enable her to explore her roots.

● The adopters could perhaps take their child to visit her country of origin or descent when she is old enough to enjoy this experience.

Children may also need help in framing an answer or "cover story" about their circumstances, to use if they are faced with questions and do not want to go into the details of their adoptive status.

The Intercountry Adoption Centre (see Tip 10) can provide more advice. Also, BAAF publishes *Adoption Coversations* (Wolfs, 2008), a guide to talking about adoption with a child who has been adopted from abroad.

Single adopters

Many single parents make excellent, resourceful adopters. The main challenge they will face in addition to the issues faced by other adopters is to ensure that they have robust support networks in place. This is, of course, important for all adopters, but for single adopters there is a particular challenge as they do not have a partner who automatically shares parental responsibility. This has implications for day-to-day care, the pressure on most single parents to work to support their child, dealing with unexpected crises, care during school holidays and the need for all parents to have a break ("me-time").

Individual adopters' situations will differ, and some will have very close relationships with extended family members or particular friends. However, there may well be times when unexpected pressures occur, where the single adopter may need to call on the local authority for support. This might mean funding some form of respite care for a period (perhaps for someone to care for the child in the home), or for financial support if circumstances (such as illness) mean a dramatic drop in income for a period. Particular attention will need to be given to these possibilities when assessing support needs.

If you are supporting a single adopter with a new placement, you could encourage him or her to make use of their support network, to arrange times to do things together with other parents and children, and also to develop a more child-centred network. This will include well-established relationships, but is also likely to include other parents met at the playgroup or the school gate. Single adopters may need encouragement to feel confident in joining in with other parents, but you should also be sensitive to the fact that the adopter might feel somewhat isolated in some situations. Single adopters may benefit from being linked up to other single adopters through a "buddying" arrangement.

Key points

- Provide support if an adopted child has particular health, emotional or behavioural difficulties. Find out what your local authority or CAMHS can offer the adopters.
- Help support the adopters and their child's education by ensuring that appropriate resources are available.
- Help adopters to liaise with their child's school to ensure that their child's behaviour is understood and can be properly managed.
- If the adopted child has a disability, be creative in working with the adopters to ascertain what form of support would be most helpful for them, and provide assistance in applying for it, if required.

- Help gay and lesbian parents to support their child by providing advice on dealing with prejudice and homophobia.
- Black and minority ethnic adopters may need help to support their child in dealing with prejudice and racism – be available to provide advice and support if necessary.
- Adopters who have adopted transracially or from overseas may require advice about helping their child to gain self-esteem and knowledge about their ethnic heritage.
- Single adopters may need support at particular times – discuss with them what form of support would be most helpful for them.

TIP 9

Be knowledgeable, creative and flexible about financial support

> *It took us ages to find out about financial help and benefits that can be available...Do as much research as possible before the child arrives.*
>
> *(Marsden, 2008, p 134)*

Financial support from the local authority

When adopters are linked with a child, the local authority has a duty to draw up a support plan which has to be agreed with the prospective adopters prior to the matching panel. The support plan will include consideration of whether there is a need for financial support. Financial support is linked to the needs of the child, not the adopters' circumstances, and is generally means-tested. (In Northern Ireland, while adoption allowances are available, the lack of support regulations means that the possibility of other financial support is very limited. However, adoptive families can apply for state benefits similar to those in the rest of the UK.)

> *It is now five years down the line and, although I undoubtedly have earning power, I'm feeling the pinch quite badly. I've accepted we will never be rich, because I am unwilling to sacrifice this important time with Alan. But we scrape by, sometimes well and sometimes not quite so well.*
>
> *(Wise, 2007, p 45)*

If adopters request financial support prior to the adoption order being made or within three years after a child has been adopted, the local authority which placed the child for adoption has a duty to assess and if appropriate, to provide financial assistance. If financial adoption support is requested later, it is the local authority where the adopters live which is responsible. Financial support can cover:

- capital expenditure on items such as a washing machine, a bigger car to accommodate several children, a wheelchair, or a loft extension to provide an extra bedroom;
- an allowance that will enable one parent to give up work and stay at home to help the child settle in for a period;
- an ongoing adoption allowance if the child has special needs such as a disability or severe emotional or behavioural difficulties, or if the parents are adopting several siblings;
- funding for respite care – in some instances, it might be appropriate for this to be residential, or it could simply enable the adopter to fund help in the home, e.g. someone skilled enough to care for a child with behavioural difficulties on a regular basis to allow the

adopters time for other essential family tasks or to have a break;

- if foster carers adopt a child in their care, enhanced allowances which match the previous fostering allowances can be paid for a period to enable the adopters to adjust to a change in income.

It is important to appreciate the financial stress that caring for adopted children can place on families and to support them to make a good case in their application for financial support. Some adopters may be reluctant to apply for this but if they can see that it will benefit their child, for example, by enabling them to spend more time at home helping them to settle in, they are more likely to feel entitled to it. (See Tip 8 for more information on supporting children with disabilities.)

MONEY MATTERS: THE COST OF RAISING A DISABLED CHILD

Dea Birkett, the mother of a 16-year-old daughter who cannot walk, wrote about the financial and other pressures on families who have a child with a disability (*The Guardian*, 28 February 2009).

- Bike for my disabled daughter, **£795**; bike for her siblings, **£79.95**
- Childcare costs for my disabled daughter, **£250** per week; childcare if we could use childminder for all three children, **£100** per week
- Cost to get to cinema for my disabled daughter, **£6** in accessible taxi; cost to get to cinema for siblings, **£0** free transport on bus
- Cost of adaptations to house, **£20,000**
- Cost of new wheelchair-accessible car, **£18,000**; cost of our old car, **£1,000**
- Cost of large-print edition of *Great Expectations* for her English GCSE, **£35**; cost of school books for siblings, **£0**
- Cost of wheelchair repairs, approximately **£70** per month
- Loss of income due to having to attend multiple appointments – immeasurable

---

Any arrangement for providing ongoing financial support will be reviewed annually or sooner if circumstances change. If the child's needs and adopters' circumstances continue to warrant the payment of financial support, it should continue for as long as the child remains with the adopters until he is aged 18 or leaves full-time education. Some local authorities are only providing financial support for a limited time. You need to be clear about your local authority's ruling and ensure that the adopters understand what is available. Adoption allowances from the local authority are not taxable.

Applying for financial support when circumstances change

Adoptive families may suffer an unexpected and sudden drop in their income, for example, due to illness, bereavement or unemployment. In other situations, the level of a child's needs may change as he grows older. The severity of a child's disability may become apparent only in later years, or emotional and behavioural difficulties that were manageable in a five-year-old may pose a much more serious management problem in a 12-year-old. As a result of such changes, a family might require financial help some years down the line, in order to maintain the child in the family.

Given that all children placed for adoption have suffered loss and broken attachments, it is a priority to ensure that the families which make the commitment of adoption are supported to continue caring for the child and providing the stability they need throughout the childhood years, as a further breakdown would inevitably be very damaging for the child.

Two-year-old Kimberley, who had learning difficulties and challenging behaviour, was placed with Rhiannon, a single parent. Rhiannon had given up her job as a nurse to care for Kimberley. Rhiannon remained at home full time for a year, after which Kimberley was enrolled in a nursery with provision for children with special needs, on a half-time basis, and Rhiannon had to return to work. With the help of her social worker, Rhiannon successfully applied to her local authority for financial support towards the cost of employing a home-based carer to look after Kimberley after nursery until she returned from work, which was much more appropriate to Kimberley's needs than full-time nursery or a busy child minder.

State-funded benefits and tax credits

Adopters are expected to claim any state benefits to which they might be entitled. Some adoptive families will never have claimed benefits before, so they may need information and support. After adopting, they will become eligible for child benefit and possibly certain other welfare benefits, tax credits and other help.

An important part of post-placement support is to make sure the family is claiming its full entitlement to financial help from the state. Some parents might appreciate their social worker's help with the task of claiming benefits and tax credits.

To apply for appropriate benefits, you have to fill out 10 different forms containing 1,194 questions, spread out over 319 pages.

Dea Birkett, mother of a child with disabilities, The Guardian, *28 February 2009*

Below are the main benefits adopters may be eligible for. Child benefit is the only universal benefit. Other benefits and tax credits depend on factors such as the person's income, savings, previous National Insurance record and/or the number of hours worked (or inability to work due to illness or disability). It is important to appreciate the financial stress that caring for adopted children can place on families and to support them to make a good case in their application.

- Child benefit (this is a universal benefit and is not means-tested)
- Child Tax Credit
- Income Support or Jobseeker's Allowance
- Working Tax Credit

- Housing benefit
- Council Tax benefit
- Employment & Support Allowance

Any financial support adopters may be receiving from their local authority which is directly related to the adoption may be taken into account in some of these benefits.

Child Trust Fund

For all children born on or after 1 September 2002, the Government will pay £250 into a Child Trust Fund account (and pay a further £250 when the child turns seven) to be administered on the child's behalf by whoever receives their child benefit. This money is to be invested and cannot be cashed before the child turns 18. Some local authorities will have claimed this on behalf of children they are looking after, and will transfer it to the adopters to administer when the child is adopted. In other cases, the adopters will need to apply once the adoption has been finalised.

If the adopted child has a disability

Another type of help that kicked in right away was William's Disability Living Allowance (DLA), to help with mobility costs and additional care arising from his disability. This is available to all children with disabilities, not just those who have been adopted.

(Marsden, 2008, p 102)

There are additional benefits (below) and schemes which provide financial help when a child has a disability. In order to be eligible, the child's disability must meet certain criteria.

- Disability Living Allowance
- Carer's Allowance
- Council Tax disability reduction

- Disabled facilities grant
- Exemption from road tax (this applies when the child is receiving the high rate of the mobility component of Disability Living Allowance)

Disability Living Allowance

If the child has a disability, Disability Living Allowance (DLA) can form a significant contribution to the family income. Conditions such as attention deficit hyperactivity disorder (ADHD), learning difficulties and Foetal Alcohol Spectrum Disorder (FASD) are now classed as disabilities, and parents who have adopted a child with these or other disabilities should be able to claim DLA. In making a claim for DLA, it is important that the applicant gives clear and detailed information about the additional support and supervision their child requires over and above what would be expected at the child's chronological age. As a social worker, you would be in a good position to give advice on this.

Motability scheme

This scheme provides a fully insured car when a child (if you are claiming on behalf of a child) gets the high rate of the mobility component of Disability Living Allowance with at least one year left to run on the award.

Funding for residential care

Some adopted adolescents may display severe behavioural difficulties related to the impact of abuse at a younger age. These may include being missing from home overnight, taking drugs, being involved in sexual activities which are potentially dangerous, and may also include threats or incidents of violence at home, either towards adopters or towards other children in the home.

In such situations, it would be important to involve the local Child and Adolescent Mental Health Services (CAMHS) and education services in a multi-agency approach to supporting the young person and the family. This may lead to therapeutic support for the adolescent being offered alongside consultation for the parents, including suggestions regarding strategies for managing conflict as well as negotiating an agreement between the young person and his parents to keep the young person safe. However, in a small number of cases, young people pose such a degree of risk to themselves or to others that the adopters may feel it not safe or sustainable for them to remain at home. Adopters may not wish the child to return to care, but may nevertheless feel that he requires more intensive support than they can realistically provide.

For some young people, a residential school, which also provides a therapeutic programme, may offer the best alternative. Such a placement need not mean that the adoption has disrupted. Adopters may benefit from the respite offered by their child attending a residential school or therapeutic community while they remain involved (albeit on the periphery for a while) as parents. This can be the most effective way to allow the young person to deal with complex emotional issues while protecting him from damaging himself and keeping the relationship with his family alive.

Inevitably, such placements are an expensive resource and applications should be considered by the local authority's resources panel, which will include representatives from the local education authority (LEA) and health services as well as children's services. By the time such an application is made, generally the various agencies have all been involved in trying to support the young person, so there is often (although not always) a willingness to find a shared solution, and to share the cost of funding it.

The post-adoption worker or ASSA is likely to have a key role in liaising with the other professionals and reminding them and agencies about the early damaging experiences the young person suffered prior to adoption which are contributing to the current difficulties. There needs to be recognition that multi-agency funding will be available only if there are supporting assessments from an education/health dimension. It is essential that professionals understand the impact of these young people's backgrounds and that the adopters have been trying to help their child recover from the impact of these experiences. If this isn't made clear, some professionals may assume that the young person's problems are a reflection of poor parenting by the adopters. Adopters often feel very much blamed for their children's emotional difficulties, which can complicate the relationship between the family and the professionals.

For more information

See the websites below for more information on financial benefits.

● www.direct.gov.uk/en/MoneyTaxAndBenefits
● www.direct.gov.uk/en/HomeAndCommunity/Yourlocalcouncil andCouncilTax/CouncilTax/DG_10037422

In many cases you can apply for benefits online.

For more information on specific benefits or to request a form, call the following helplines.

● Child benefit: 0845 302 1444
● Housing benefit, Council Tax benefit, Council Tax Disability Reduction, Disabled Facilities Grant: contact the appropriate local authority
● Income Support, Jobseeker's Allowance, Employment & Support Allowance: 0800 055 6688
● Child Tax Credit, Working Tax Credit: 0845 300 3900
● Disabled Living Allowance, Carer's Allowance: 0800 882200
● Exemption from road tax: 0845 712 3456
● Motability: 0845 456 4566
● Child Trust Fund: 0845 302 1470

Key points

● Encourage adopters to apply for appropriate financial support from the local authority – this will benefit the child and the placement. Also ensure they are aware that they can re-apply (or apply for the first time) later on, if circumstances or the child's needs change.
● Ensure adopters are aware of any state benefits that they may be entitled to, and provide advice about applying for these.

TIP 10

Build your knowledge of resources for adopters

Last year William's OT decided that he would benefit from a specialist tricycle. She produced a brochure and we noticed that it would cost about £1,000. 'But don't worry,' she said, 'I'll try and get some financial help from a Trust.' We filled in various forms and gave details of our income, and to our surprise a Trust did come up with the funding.

(Marsden, 2008, p 109)

There are national organisations which are an important source of help and support to adopters and other parents. Many of these are listed below.

However, many of the resources that are most useful will be local. You can help adoptive parents by building up your own knowledge of these local contacts and organisations that both you and they can call on for support of various kinds. Health and education are both likely to be important issues. Your role is to act as an advocate for the adoptive family and support them in getting the help they need, but to allow them to take the lead role in this.

You need to know where your local CAMHS service is based, and what their referral process is. Some local authorities have a protocol for referring looked after and adopted children to CAMHS. If this does not exist in your area, it may be something to suggest to the Adoption Support Services Adviser (ASSA) in your agency.

Each school will have a SENCO and most local authorities will have an educational psychologist for looked after children. Either of these would be a helpful place to start in thinking about meeting a child's needs in the school setting.

Adoption Support Services Adviser (ASSA)

In England and Wales, each local authority adoption team will have an ASSA and this person will play an important role in helping you to identify resources and services that could help the adoptive family. In Scotland and Northern Ireland, an adoption support worker should undertake a similar role. The ASSA also has the responsibility of liaising with the PCT and LEA regarding adoption support services.

Local groups for peer support

Adoption UK is a national organisation supporting adoptive families and adopted people. It has local groups, internet message boards and a journal for members. It would be useful for your adopters to know whether Adoption UK runs a support group in their area.

A number of local authorities and adoption consortia run support groups for adopters, or parenting support groups particularly geared towards adopters – this is another avenue to investigate which could be useful for your adopters.

Adoption support organisations

There are a number of adoption support organisations throughout the UK which adopters can contact for advice and information. The Consortium of Adoption Support Agencies (CASA), a group set up to bring together agencies providing adoption support services, lists contact details for a number of these on their website at www.casa-uk.org.

Useful organisations

Adoption UK
Linden House, 55 The Green
South Bar Street
Banbury
Oxfordshire OX16 9AB
Helpline: 0844 848 7900
Tel: 01295 752240
www.adoptionuk/org

British Association for Adoption & Fostering (BAAF)
Head Office
Saffron House
6–10 Kirby Street
London EC1N 8TS
Tel: 020 7421 2600
www.baaf.org.uk

BAAF Scotland
113 Rose Street
Edinburgh EH2 3DT
Tel: 0131 226 9270

BAAF Cymru
7 Cleeve House
Lambourne Crescent
Cardiff CF14 5GP
Tel: 029 2076 1155

BAAF Northern Ireland
Botanic House
1–5 Botanic Avenue
Belfast BT7 1JG
Tel: 028 9031 5494

Pink Parents
A support group for lesbians and gay men who are considering
parenting, adopting or fostering, or who have children in their
extended family.
Unit 29 Hillier Road
Devizes
Wiltshire SN10 2FB
Tel: 01380 727935
www.pinkparents.org.uk

**Northern Support Group for Lesbian and Gay Foster and
Adoptive Parents**
A support group based in the North of England, for lesbian and gay
foster carers and adopters.
Tel: 07949 254620
www.nsgroup.org.uk/

New Family Social
A UK online network for lesbian and gay adopters.
Tel: 0843 289 9457
www.newfamilysocial.co.uk

www.direct.gov.uk
Provides information on a range of public services, including for
children with disabilities, special educational needs and support at
school.

Contact a Family
A UK-wide charity which provides advice, information and support
for all families with disabled children, including linking families with
disabled children with others whose children have the same
impairment. Its online forum, www.makingcontact.org, includes a
searchable database of over 2,000 conditions, with information and
details of support groups.

209–211 City Road
London EC1V 1JN
Tel: 020 7608 8700
www.cafamily.org.uk

Face 2 Face Network
A befriending service for parents of children with a special need or disability, this network has schemes across the UK for anyone whose child has been recognised as having a long-term disability. If there is no scheme in your area, email or phone contact can be arranged with trained befrienders.
Tel: 0844 800 9189
www.face2facenetwork.org.uk

Advisory Centre for Education
Offers guidance to parents and others on all aspects of school education.
Tel: 0808 800 5793 (Advice 2pm–5pm)
www.ace-ed.org.uk

Independent Panel for Special Education Advice
Legally-based advice and support for parents about special educational needs and disability discrimination at school.
Tel: 0800 018 4016 Mon–Fri 10am–4pm
www.ipsea.org.uk

Intercountry Adoption Centre
Provides advice and information to prospective adopters and social workers involved in intercountry adoption, including information days, post-adoption workshops and an advice line.
64–66 High Street
Barnet
Herts EN5 5SJ
Advice line: 0870 516 8742
Tel: 020 8449 2562
www.icacentre.org.uk

See Tip 9 for sources of information about financial matters and benefits.

Afterword:
A personal experience of adoption support

My wife and I adopted two children, brother and sister aged six and seven. It was the start of a radically new life for us all. In the following years, we hung on to the endless rollercoaster of emotions, bureaucracy and uncertainty that is adoptive family life. Over the years since then, all of us have changed; all of us almost reached breaking point; all of us feel we have come through the stronger. Parenting our two children has often been difficult, often wonderful, but then we've seen other parents struggle and wonder at their children. The social workers we've worked with have supported us as individuals and parents, as well as adopters.

We were together for 15 years when we got married, in our forties, and tried for children of our own. The investigations and IVF were painful, emotionally and physically, but we supported each other and had the support of our friends and family. We realised that parenting was more important than conceiving, so started to explore adoption.

Our local authority social workers were swamped with emergency placements and helpfully recommended seeking approval via a voluntary adoption agency. We met several, choosing Coram because they had a "grown-up" attitude to us: from the start, they recognised our commitment, were realistic about likely placements and objectively supported our application.

At Coram's discussion groups, we met others in the same ocean of uncertainty. We read the *Be My Parent* newspaper's profiles, full of jargon, the huge range of life stories – particularly for older children seeking adoption. With too much information and emotion, we desperately held onto Coram's social workers' objectivity, realism and optimism. It echoed our hope and shored up our confidence in our parenting ability. It made us realise how important it was for us to be very open with each other, so we would go into this truly together.

The approvals process – which took about nine months, inevitably – was completely surreal. With both of us working full time, trying to hold together "normal life", we were constantly asked by "our" social worker to look back to our pasts and forward to being a family, and to relate them. Through it all, she was our confidante, coach, tormentor, and guide to the bureaucracy and legal process.

I'm glad that approval took that long, it was a lot to think through: what sort of children would we prefer; how many of them; our anticipated daily routine with "the kids"; our policy on discipline; where would they sleep; what happens if they get sick; what do we tell the neighbours? This process shaped our family's future. Who was going to stay at home and look after the kids? We decided that I would be the stay-at-home dad – probably the best decision I've ever taken! Coram supported that too, making sure we'd explored all the implications together.

Approval itself in the November before we adopted in July was – at least for us – no big deal. We knew our social worker thought we were ready. We read our Form F and were amazed to hear about these people who would be parents: they sounded OK (and they sounded like us). We didn't feel any need to go to panel. Then we were waiting for matching.

Unbeknownst to us, our future children – let's call them David and Fiona – had their own journey to adoption. Their parents – let's call them Wendy and Gordon – were a young, white, middle-class couple in loving families of their own. Nonetheless, they struggled to look after David when he came and were more or less defeated when the second child Fiona arrived, less than a year later. Wendy, in particular, was fiercely independent and emotionally unstable, making it difficult for them to get support from relatives. Quite quickly, Fiona was failing to thrive and on the "at risk" register. David was unduly quiet and witnessed domestic violence. Gordon lost his job and left the home for good, leaving Wendy to bring up the babies.

When Wendy was assessed as unable to cope, the children were put into emergency foster placements and care plans drawn up. The grandparents offered a more active role in looking after the toddlers but then withdrew, so eventually David and Fiona went into voluntary long-term foster care, with a view to adoption. The foster carers had children of their own and several foster children. For 18 months they looked after David and Fiona and gave them the stability they needed (after three previous foster placements and five different schools). Our kids still look back at the foster house as their favourite place. We later heard that during the previous autumn, they had been matched with a couple but Wendy had withdrawn her support for adoption so the matching stopped. Social services decided to apply for a freeing order and re-advertised the children, which is when Coram heard of them.

We heard about "our two" in the January after our approval. Our social worker had been suggesting children for us to consider – very helpful, as we had no idea how to choose between all the children that seemed from their profiles to be OK for us. I remember reading half a dozen Form Es in a hotel in Amsterdam and crying at the heartbreaking stories and my inability to choose between them. Our social worker was able to de-jargon the descriptions and give examples of the likely impact on the children of their histories.

We saw the first three photos of our two, standing on a five-bar gate at the farm, and were smitten. Their adoption story seemed a combination of bungling and selfishness, rather than great harm – we couldn't understand how two such seemingly ordinary, beautiful, charming children would need adopting, when they had such seemingly ordinary, capable and loving relatives. Nonetheless, we all came to believe they would have the best chance for the future with us.

They lived hundreds of miles away, so their whole social worker team, their female foster carer and two of Coram's social workers (including ours, of course) came to meet us. The foster carer was fiercely loving of the children, presenting a "warts and all" picture of them which proved to be the most useful information about them we received. We spent hours together after the meeting, coming down from it with our social worker. Most unnerving of all was the need to get the "freeing order" for the children before the placement could happen.

In early July, that order came through and suddenly we were to have the children placed with us by the end of July. We exchanged videos and photo albums and then travelled up to meet them. I was numb with apprehension. The planning meeting was where we negotiated – with Coram's help – a series of scheduled contact meetings, starting that afternoon. The foster carer picked them up from school. Fiona was supposed to be the chatty one and David very quiet, but they came in and saw us and it was David whose smile lit the room, who took us on a tour of their farm, with Fiona hiding behind the foster carer's legs.

We spent one week up near them and then a couple of weekends, getting to know them. We still tell each other stories of the time before placement, the boundaries they pushed, such as when we took them to a restaurant and they hid in the toilets to see if we would come looking for them. Or the children showing off their toys, us putting them to bed, but them not allowing us to put a plaster on a cut. Or when they came to stay with us overnight, were so excited they wouldn't go to sleep in bed and fell asleep in our laps very late that night.

We had four-hour nightly discussions and then phone calls with our social worker, trying to make sense of each day's events. In one discussion, my wife pointed out to me that the children hadn't spoken to her all day. I'd been taken up with the attention they were lavishing on me and failed to spot they (and I) were completely ignoring her. Divide and rule played out right under my nose! We agreed that night to speak as one voice even when apart, which stands us in good stead to this day. Our social worker was a point of sanity, constantly reassuring us that this was normal behaviour and that we were coping very well.

Then the day came when we loaded up our car with them (and their toys), drove for hours back to our house and realised they were with us to stay for ever. After that, it became a really wild ride! I'd thought that everything would be OK once we'd got the children placed with us. Coram had said that placement was just the beginning, a bit like birth – that's when the fun begins. But I'd given up my "full-on" job, thought I'd have more time on my hands and had several projects in mind to do when the kids were playing quietly by themselves. In retrospect, we were very lucky that my wife could take weeks of adoption leave and that the kids weren't jumping from one school straight into another – we had the whole summer to get to know each other. Because, from day one, we were in a completely different reality.

Being older, at seven and six, both David and Fiona voiced their opinions on everything but they weren't able to get much beyond like or don't like. We were advised to provide familiar food, routines, activities, even shampoo: but they didn't know how to tell us what these were. I'd ask, 'How do you want your eggs?'; they would reply, 'I want normal eggs'. Phone calls to the foster carer and our social worker gave clarification on whether they had in fact been able to swim a mile (no) or drive a motorbike (no) or had had asthma (no), liked their eggs fried (yes), were allergic to antibiotics (yes) or broccoli (no), or had a pet lamb (yes).

We also had to find them a school place in six weeks. We had been told they were between one and two years academically delayed. Our preferred primary school was full – so we got Coram on the case. Our social worker wrote to the school in support of our (unsuccessful) appeal and gave us guidance on choosing a more suitable school. She also advised us about what the kids could tell their peers (and the children of our neighbours) about their backgrounds. We chose a different local primary, where they could go together and which had a more positive attitude to kids with educational needs. Later on, she advised us about dealing with David's anger and Fiona's low self-esteem, as these came to light.

Both children were initially reluctant to allow us to parent them – David took himself to the bathroom one night to throw up, Fiona refused cuddles even when upset. However, while seemingly fiercely independent, they both went through several months of regression. Fiona began wearing nappies, acquiring baby equipment and generally being a toddler. She wanted a cot for her birthday, chose her own bottles, used a pacifier and yearned for a buggy big enough for her. We talked these through with Coram as they came up and realised that Fiona wasn't just "playing" – she needed to do this with us. With Coram's guidance, we drew up boundaries together to protect Fiona from ridicule: no nappies or bottles outside the house; David not to tell tales about her baby behaviour; toddler tantrums only at home. She amazed us by being able to separate quite clearly her toddler behaviour from her six-year-old behaviour. David tried out the buggy, briefly wore a nappy and play-acted toddler behaviour, but for him it was much more play than necessity.

Fiona's slow attachment to my wife was something we also discussed at length with our social worker. She described the emotions Fiona might have been having regarding her fear of further betrayal by her new mum, cautioned against taking Fiona's anger personally, said Fiona wouldn't be pushing boundaries unless she felt safe and secure. We hung on to these thoughts through the rough times in the first couple of years.

Contact arrangements didn't entirely help matters. When freed, the court recommended that both children have twice-yearly contact with Wendy, if in their best interest. We were supportive of the idea, although cautious about the practicalities and possible adverse impact on their attachment to us. We met Wendy during the introduction week, with our social worker. Wendy said she believed adoption with us was the best thing for her children. However, at her farewell meeting she told the kids she hoped they would be coming back to live with her again.

These confusing messages gave us some concern, but we agreed to the initial contact six months after the kids were placed. Our social worker negotiated the terms of the contact: Wendy was to travel down with her parents and social worker; certain things were not to be discussed; only certain presents and photos were allowed. Coram's safe and controlled contact venue was offered. She checked these with the children's social workers. We told the children the week before contact – as advised by Coram. They were very excited and pleased. We took them to see the venue, so they would be familiar with it. Then, on the Friday before the Monday contact, Coram was called by Wendy's social worker, saying Wendy was unwell, didn't accept the terms of the contact and couldn't come, and neither could her parents – so contact was off.

I think that significantly delayed our children's attachment to us. The children were angry and worried at Wendy being ill – David, in particular, wanted to go and help make her better. Our social worker came round to give them the news, so it wasn't just us saying it, and arranged an urgent case review. We agreed to try contact with Wendy or her parents one more time, and it went better but not as we had hoped.

We now have meetings approximately annually with Wendy's parents. Coram facilitates the meetings, contacting the birth family's social services in preparation. Contact can still be disruptive, but as the children have got older, they are better able to cope.

The last formal contact with our social worker was the adoption hearing – she had been with us for two years. The hearing was scheduled for the High Court in London. Despite being very settled with us for a long time, the children were nervous that they wouldn't be allowed to stay with us. Our social worker once again held us together, pre-empting some of the likely concerns and keeping us one step ahead of our emotions. The day itself was a suitably grand and moving event, and a great deal of fun too. It had a huge impact on the kids – they were more relaxed in the weeks afterwards.

Now they are teenagers – with all that entails. The best way to describe them is just like their peers in most ways: perhaps a bit more cautious, less adventurous; perhaps a bit more likely to misinterpret friendships; perhaps a bit less likely to ask for help.

We still chat with Coram occasionally, checking out that what's going on in our lives is "normal": thankfully, so far it is.

Bibliography

Archer C (1999a) *First Steps in Parenting the Child who Hurts: Tiddlers and toddlers*, London: Jessica Kingsley Publishers

Archer A (1999b) *Next Steps in Parenting the Child who Hurts: Tykes and teens*, London: Jessica Kingsley Publishers

Argent H (2004) *Related by Adoption*, London: BAAF

Bingley Miller L and Bentovim A (2007) *Adopted Children and their Families: Building secure new lives*, London: Routledge

Bond H (2007) *Ten Top Tips for Managing Contact*, London: BAAF

Carr K (2007) *Adoption Undone*, London: BAAF

Department for Education and Skills (2005a) *Adoption Support Services Regulations*, London: DfES

Department for Education and Skills (2005b) *Practice Guidance on Assessing the Support Needs of Adoptive Families*, London: DfES

Fahlberg V (1994) *A Child's Journey Through Placement*, London: BAAF

Henderson K and Sargent N (2005) 'Developing the Incredible Years Webster-Stratton parenting skills training programme for use with adoptive families', *Adoption & Fostering*, 29:4, pp 34–44

Hill N (2009) *The Pink Guide to Adoption for Lesbians and Gay Men*, London: BAAF

Hirst M (2005) *Loving and Living with Traumatised Children: Reflections by adoptive parents*, London: BAAF

Howe D (1996a) *Adopters on Adoption: Reflections on parenthood and children*, London: BAAF

Howe D (1996b) 'Adopters' relationships with their adopted children from adolescence to early adulthood', *Adoption & Fostering*, 20:3, pp35–43

Howe D (1998) *Patterns of Adoption: Nature, nurture and psychosocial development*, London: Blackwell Science

Jewett C (1994) *Helping Children Cope with Separation and Loss*, London: BAAF

Keck G (2009) *Parenting Adopted Adolescents: Understanding and appreciating their journeys*, Colorado Springs, CO: Navpress Press

Keck G and Kupecky R (2009) *Parenting the Hurt Child: Helping adoptive families heal and grow*, Colorado Springs, CO: Navpress Press

Loxterkamp L (2009) 'Contact and truth: the unfolding predicament in adoption and fostering', *Clinical Child Psychology and Psychiatry*, 14:3, pp 423–435

Marsden R (2008) *The Family Business*, London: BAAF

Pallett C, Blackeby K, Yule W, Weissman R and Scott S (2005) *Fostering Changes: How to improve relationships and manage difficult behaviour*, London: BAAF

Pallett C, Blackeby K, Yule W, Weissman R and Scott S with Fursland F (2008) *Managing Difficult Behaviour: A handbook for foster carers of the under-12s*, London: BAAF

Performance and Innovation Unit (2000) *Prime Minister's Review: Adoption*, London: Performance and Innovation Unit

Prior V and Glaser D (2006) *Understanding Attachment and Attachment Disorders*, London: Jessica Kingsley Publishers

Rees J (2009) *Life Story Books: A family-friendly approach*, London: Jessica Kingsley Publishers

Royce R and Royce E (2008) *Together in Time*, London: BAAF

Rushton A (2008) 'Adoption support', in Schofield G and Simmonds J, *The Child Placement Handbook*, London: BAAF, pp 260–275

Rushton A and Monck E (2009) *Enhancing Adoptive Parenting: A test of effectiveness*, London: BAAF

Sturge-Moore L (ed) (2005) *Could you be my Parent? Adoption and fostering stories*, London: BAAF

Sturgess W and Selwyn J (2007) 'Supporting the placements of children adopted out of care', *Clinical Child Psychology and Psychiatry*, 12:1, pp 13–28

Sunderland M (2006) *What Every Parent Needs to Know: The remarkable effects of love, nurture and play on your child's development*, London: Dorling Kindersley

Webster-Stratton C (2006) *The Incredible Years: A trouble shooting guide for parents of children aged 2-8 years* (2nd edn), Seattle, WA: Webster-Stratton

Wise J (2007) *Flying Solo*, London: BAAF

Useful books for adopters

Hill N (2009) *The Pink Guide to Adoption for Lesbians and Gay Men*, London: BAAF

Massiah H (ed) (2005) *Looking After our Own: The stories of black and Asian adopters*, London: BAAF

Morrison M (2007) *Talking about Adoption to your Adopted Child: A guide for adoptive parents*, London: BAAF

Salter AN (2006) *The Adopter's Handbook: Information, resources and services for adoptive parents*, London: BAAF

Wolfs R (2008) *Adoption Conversations: What, when and how to tell*, London: BAAF

BAAF also publishes the Our Story series of personal narratives which tell the stories of adopters and foster carers. Many of these titles would be of interest to adopters.